TEACHER'S PET PUBLICATIONS

LITPLAN TEACHER PACK
for
Antigone
based on the play by
Sophocles

Written by
Susan R. Woodward

© 2006 Teacher's Pet Publications
All Rights Reserved

This **LitPlan** for *Antigone*

has been brought to you by Teacher's Pet Publications, Inc.

Copyright Teacher's Pet Publications, Inc. 2006

Only the student materials in this unit plan (such as worksheets, study questions, and tests) may be reproduced multiple times for use in the purchaser's classroom.

For any additional copyright questions,
contact Teacher's Pet Publications, Inc..

www.tpet.com

TABLE OF CONTENTS – *Antigone LitPlan*

Introduction	6
Unit Objectives	8
Reading Assignment Sheet	9
Unit Outline	10
Study Questions (Short Answer)	13
Answer Key (Short Answer)	16
Quiz/Study Questions (Multiple Choice)	23
Answer Key (Multiple Choice)	37
Pre-reading Vocabulary Worksheets	41
Answer Key (Vocabulary Worksheets)	53
Lesson One (Introductory Lesson)	57
Writing Assignment 1: Mythological Tragedies	60
Nonfiction Assignment Sheet	62
Oral Reading Evaluation Form	64
Peer Edit Form: Writing Tragedies	66
Writing Assignment 2: Life of Sophocles	71
Writing Evaluation Form	72
Vocabulary Review Activities	79
Extra Writing Assignments/Discussion ?s	81
Writing Assignment 3: Moral Dilemmas	84
Group Presentation Evaluation Sheet	87
Unit Review Activities	88
Unit Tests	93
Unit Resource Materials	131
Vocabulary Resource Materials	147

A FEW NOTES ABOUT THE AUTHOR: SOPHOCLES

Sophocles was born in Colonus, a small town outside of Athens, Greece in 495 B.C. He was the son of an armor manufacturer who became schooled in poetry, music, and dancing. He was prized for his exceptional physique and abilities in the arts. When he was fifteen years old, Sophocles earned his reputation as a performer when he was selected to lead a chorus of boys in the paean (a hymn of victory and thanksgiving to the gods) after the battle of Salamis. He went on to become an established playwright in Athens, authoring more than 120 plays.

Sophocles first public recognition as a playwright came when he won first prize at the festival of Dionysus (called the *Dionysia*) in 468 B.C. At these festivals, playwrights were to complete three tragedies and one satyr-play (collectively, this was called a *tetralogy;* "tetra" means "four"). This particular festival's outcome was significant for his career because the twenty-eight year old Sophocles won the coveted prize over Athens' established playwright, Aeschylus. As the years continued, Sophocles went on to win first prize a total of twenty-four times (since each tetralogy consisted of four plays, he wrote ninety-six first place award winning plays), and seven second place awards out of the thirty-one competitions he entered. Sadly, out of over one hundred twenty plays written by Sophocles, only seven still exist in their entirety. These are:

Ajax	445 B.C.
Antigone	440 B.C.
Electra	440 B.C.
Oedipus Rex	430 B.C.
The Trachiniae	413 B.C.
Philoctetes	410 B.C.
Odeipus at Colonus	401 B.C. (date of first performance; five years after the death of Sophocles)

Although the Oedipus plays (*Oedipus Rex, Oedipus at Colonus,* and *Antigone)* are commonly thought of as a trilogy, they were not written as such (see above dates). Also, since there are inconsistencies in characterizations and events between them, the plays are best studied as individual works rather than part of a trilogy.

Sophocles was also involved in the technical aspect of the Greek theatre as well. He introduced the idea of painted scenery, variations in the types of music sung by the chorus, as well as increasing the size of the cast: the chorus went from twelve members to fifteen, and the number of actors in a production increased from two to three. The elaborate costumes (especially the masks) allowed the actors to portray numerous characters throughout the production. With the addition of a third actor on the stage, plot development and distinguishing between characters became more comprehensive to the audiences.

Although most of Sophocles' life centered on theatre and writing (he also wrote poetry), he was also involved at a civic level. He served as a general under Pericles in the army and was a key negotiator in the Peloponnesian War. In his role as a priest, Sophocles was concerned with the individual's need to find his/her own place in the moral and cosmic order of the universe. His plays contain moral lessons that usually pertain to man's duty to the gods and the avoidance of excessive pride. Late in life, Sophocles acted as a statesman who helped organize the recovery of Athens after it was defeated at Syracuse.

Sophocles was said to have been especially blessed by the gods, and he was highly revered in his society. His physical beauty, strength, sense of fairness, and talent earned him the admiration of those around him, and upon his death in 406 B.C., Athens mourned. A shrine, called *Dexion* (The Entertainer) was established in his honor, and annual sacrifices were offered in his memory.

INTRODUCTION

This LitPlan has been designed to develop students' reading, writing, thinking, and language skills through exercises and activities related to *Antigone*. It includes 19 lessons, supported by extra resource materials.

The **introductory lesson** introduces students to Greek Mythology and the Greek Theatre. Following the introductory activity, students are given a transition to explain how the activity relates to the play they are about to read. Following the transition, students are given the materials they will be using during the unit. At the end of the lesson, students begin the pre-reading work for the first reading assignment.

The **reading assignments** are approximately fifteen to twenty pages each; some are a little shorter while others are a little longer. Students have approximately 15 minutes of pre-reading work to do prior to each reading assignment. This pre-reading work involves reviewing the study questions for the assignment and doing some vocabulary work for 10 vocabulary words they will encounter in their reading.

The **study guide questions** are fact-based questions; students can find the answers to these questions right in the text. These questions come in two formats: short answer or multiple choice. The best use of these materials is probably to use the short answer version of the questions as study guides for students (since answers will be more complete), and to use the multiple choice version for occasional quizzes.

The **vocabulary work** is intended to enrich students' vocabularies as well as to aid in the students' understanding of the play. Prior to each reading assignment, students will complete a two-part worksheet for 10 vocabulary words in the upcoming reading assignment. Part I focuses on students' use of general knowledge and contextual clues by giving the sentence in which the word appears in the text. Students are then to write down what they think the words mean based on the words' usage. Part II nails down the definitions of the words by giving students dictionary definitions of the words and having students match the words to the correct definitions based on the words' contextual usage. Students should then have an understanding of the words when they meet them in the text.

After each reading assignment, students will go back and formulate answers for the study guide questions. Discussion of these questions serves as a **review** of the most important events and ideas presented in the reading assignments.

After students complete reading the work, there is a **vocabulary review** lesson which pulls together all of the fragmented vocabulary lists for the reading assignments and gives students a review of all of the words they have studied.

Following the vocabulary review, a lesson is devoted to the **extra discussion questions/writing assignments**. These questions focus on interpretation, critical analysis and personal response, employing a variety of thinking skills and adding to the students' understanding of the play.

There is a **group writing project** in this unit (this is part of the three writing assignments listed below). Student groups will select a mythological story from a select list, and they will create a Greek Tragedy based on the myth following the format of *Antigone*. This will include composing odes and making masks.

There are three **writing assignments** in this unit, each with the purpose of informing, persuading, or having students express personal opinions.
1. Students will research the life of Sophocles. (He was more than a playwright.)
2. Students will be presented with a moral dilemma and will have to present both sides of the situation and then attempt to persuade the reader of the validity of their position in the dilemma.
3. Students will write their own Greek tragedies (following the format of *Antigone*) based on a Greek myth.

There is a **nonfiction reading assignment**. Students must read nonfiction articles, books, etc. to gather information about the history of Greek Theatre.

The **review lesson** pulls together all of the aspects of the unit. The teacher is given several choices of activities or games to use which all serve the same basic function of reviewing all of the information presented in the unit.

The **unit test** comes in two formats: multiple choice or short answer. As a convenience, two different tests for each format have been included. There is also an advanced short answer unit test for advanced students.

There are additional **support materials** included with this unit. The **Unit Resource Materials** section includes suggestions for an in-class library, crossword and word search puzzles related to the play, and extra worksheets. There is a list of **bulletin board ideas** which gives the teacher suggestions for bulletin boards to go along with this unit. In addition, there is a list of **extra class activities** the teacher could choose from to enhance the unit or as a substitution for an exercise the teacher might feel is inappropriate for his/her class. **Answer keys** are located directly after the **reproducible student materials** throughout the unit. The **Vocabulary Resource Materials** section includes similar worksheets and games to reinforce the vocabulary words.

The **level** of this unit can be varied depending upon the criteria on which the individual assignments are graded, the teacher's expectations of his/her students in class discussions, and the formats chosen for the study guides, quizzes and test. If teachers have other ideas/activities they wish to use, they can usually easily be inserted prior to the review lesson.

The student materials may be reproduced for use in the teacher's classroom without infringement of copyrights. No other portion of this unit may be reproduced without the written consent of Teacher's Pet Publications, Inc.

UNIT OBJECTIVES - *Antigone*

1. Through reading Sophocles' *Antigone*, students will learn about the history of Greek Theatre and the structure of a Greek Tragedy, as well as about the life of the playwright, Sophocles.

2. Students will complete a project in a cooperative group.

3. Students will demonstrate their understanding of the text on four levels: factual, interpretive, critical and personal.

4. Students will explore the themes of love, devotion to one's god as opposed to the subservience of the law, compassion, and making choices.

5. Students will be given the opportunity to practice reading both aloud and silently to improve their skills in each area.

6. Students will answer questions to demonstrate their knowledge and understanding of the main events and characters in *Antigone* as they relate to the playwright's theme development.

7. Students will enrich their vocabularies and improve their understanding of the play through the vocabulary lessons prepared for use in conjunction with the play.

8. The writing assignments in this unit are designed for several purposes:
    a. To have students demonstrate their abilities to inform, to persuade, or to express their own personal ideas
    Note: Students will demonstrate the ability to write effectively <u>to inform</u> by developing and organizing facts to convey information. Students will demonstrate the ability to write effectively to <u>persuade</u> by selecting and organizing relevant information, establishing an argumentative purpose, and by designing an appropriate strategy for an identified audience. Students will demonstrate the ability to write effectively to <u>express personal ideas</u> by selecting a form and its appropriate elements.
    b. To check the students' reading comprehension
    c. To make students think about the ideas presented by the play
    d. To encourage logical thinking
    e. To provide an opportunity to practice good grammar and improve students' use of the English language.

9. Students will read aloud, report, and participate in large and small group discussions to improve their public speaking and personal interaction skills.

READING ASSIGNMENT SHEET - *Antigone*

Date Assigned	Scenes Assigned	Date Completed
	Prologue and Parodos	
	Scene 1 and Ode 1	
	Scene 2 and Ode 2	
	Scene 3 and Ode 3	
	Scene 4 and Ode 4	
	Scene 5	
	Paean and Exodos	

UNIT OUTLINE – *Antigone*

1	2	3	4	5
Greek Mythology Background: assign interpretive writing project Intro to Greek Theatre	PVR Prologue and Parodos Oedipus background Media center visit: non-fiction assignment	Study ?s Prologue and Parodos Read aloud/perform Prologue-Ode 1 PVR Scene1/Ode 1	Study ?s Scene 1 and Ode 1 Quiz: Prologue-Ode 1 Peer Edit PVR Scene2/Ode 2	Study ?s Scene 2 and Ode 2. Read aloud/perform Scene 2-Ode 3 Mask Making PVR Scene3/Ode 3
6 Study ?s Scene 3 and Ode 3 Quiz: Scene/Odes 2 and 3 Characterization posters PVR Scene4/Ode 4	**7** Study ?s Scene 4 and Ode 4 Media center visit: Informational Writing Assignment Sophocles PVR Scene 5	**8** Study ?s Scene 5 Read aloud/perform Scene 4- Exodos PVR Paean and Exodos	**9** Study ?s Paean and Exodos Power of persuasion Quiz Scene 4 - Exodos.	**10** <u>Odes</u> - define and read "Ode to a Grecian Urn" - examine Odes 1-4 for figurative language - write odes for group tragedies
11 Group Work: completing the tragedies	**12** Vocabulary Work	**13** Group Work: Extra Discussion Questions	**14** In-Class Writing: Persuasion Piece Moral Dilemma	**15** Peer Editing: Persuasion Piece Moral Dilemma
16 Presentations of Tragedies Day 1	**17** Presentation of Tragedies Day 2	**18** Review Materials	**19** Unit Test	**20**

Key: P = Preview Study Questions   V = Vocabulary Work   R = Read

STUDY GUIDE QUESTIONS

SHORT ANSWER STUDY GUIDE QUESTIONS - *Antigone*

Prologue and Parodos:
1. How are Antigone and Ismene related?
2. Who are the two brothers mentioned in the prologue?
3. How did the two brothers die?
4. What is King Creon's decree?
5. What does Antigone plan to do?
6. What is Ismene's decision regarding the King's decree?
7. What does the Choragos compare Polyneices to in the Parodos?
8. What city has "seven gates in a yawning ring"?
9. What does the Chorus compare Thebes to?
10. According to the Choragos, what does God hate?

Scene 1 and Ode 1:
1. Who is the new King of Thebes?
2. How did the new King of Thebes claim heir to the throne?
3. What crime has Ployneices committed in the opinion of the king?
4. What news does the sentry bring to Creon?
5. How was it decided which of the sentries would bring the news about Polyneices to Creon?
6. How does Creon believe the act of burying Polyneices was carried out?
7. What does Creon demand that the sentry do?
8. According to Ode 1, what is the most wonderful of all the world's wonders?
9. Of all the winds, man has made himself secure against all except one. Which wind is that?
10. List man's accomplishments according to Ode 1.

Scene 2 and Ode 2:
1. Who has the sentry captured and brought before King Creon?
2. How did the guards manage to capture Antigone?
3. How did Antigone react to being captured by the sentries?
4. What reason does Antigone give for defying Creon's decree?
5. Who else does Creon have arrested in connection with the crime of burying Polyneices?
6. Why is Antigone angry with Ismene?
7. Besides being Antigone's uncle, how else were Creon and Antigone related?
8. What is to be Antigone's punishment for burying her brother?
9. According to Ode 2, who is the fortunate man?
10. Who is the god who must not be made angry, according to Ode 2?

Antigone Study Guide Questions

Scene 3 and Ode 3:
1. What is Haimon's initial response when his father asks how he feels about the king's decision to execute Antigone?
2. What does Creon say that men pray for?
3. Why is Creon intent on harshly punishing, even family members, all those who break the law?
4. What does Haimon claim is God's crowning gift to man?
5. What does Haimon tell King Creon about the people of Thebes' allegiance to him?
6. Whose point, King Creon's or Haimon's, does the Choragos support?
7. How does the city feel about Antigone's crime?
8. While Creon is ranting at his son, what does the king threaten to do?
9. Describe Creon's death sentence for Antigone.
10. According to Ode 3, what is it that "even the pure Immortals cannot escape"?

Scene 4 and Ode 4:
1. Whose fate does Antigone compare to her own?
2. What does Antigone beg the people of Thebes to bear witness to?
3. Who does Antigone blame for her terrible misfortune?
4. According to the chorus, what is considered a virtue?
5. What does Creon sarcastically say would have man singing forever?
6. According to Ode 4, who was locked away in a brazen vault?
7. Who came to the princess while she was locked away?
8. Who "bore the gods' prisoning anger for his pride"?
9. What is the "half remembered tale of horror" that old men tell?
10. Who, as a child, had "raced with young colts on the glittering hills/And walked untrammeled in open light"?

Scene 5:
1. Who is the blind prophet who comes to speak to King Creon?
2. What does the prophet claim that he heard which frightened him?
3. What happened when the prophet began "the rites of burnt-offering at the altar"?
4. What does the prophet claim to be the cause of the gods' reaction to their offerings?
5. What does the prophet claim can be done to repair the evil performed against the gods?
6. What is King Creon's reaction to Teiresias' message?
7. What is it that Creon claims all prophets love?
8. What warning does Teiresias give to King Creon if he refuses to heed the prophesies?
9. What advice does the Choragos give King Creon once Teiresias leaves?
10. How does King Creon react to the advice of the Choragos?

Antigone Study Guide Questions

Paean and Exodos:
1. The Choragos and the Chorus pray to a "God of many names". What are some of these names?
2. Who does the messenger claim is "a walking dead man"?
3. How has Teiresias' prophecy that Creon would pay to the gods "flesh of [his] own flesh" come true?
4. Who is Eurydice?
5. What were Creon and the messenger doing when they prayed to Hecate and Pluto?
6. What did King Creon and the messenger do as soon as they finished their tasks regarding Polyneices?
7. Describe what Creon saw when he looked through the crevice into Antigone's tomb.
8. Describe Haimon's reaction when Creon entered Antigone's tomb.
9. What happened after the messenger relayed the news about Haimon and Antigone to Eurydice?
10. What does the Choragos claim is "always punished" by the gods?

ANSWER KEY SHORT ANSWER STUDY GUIDE QUESTIONS - *Antigone*

Prologue and Parodos:

1. How are Antigone and Ismene related?
   They are sisters, the daughters of Oedipus.

2. Who are the two brothers mentioned in the prologue?
   They are the brothers of Antigone and Ismene: Eteocles and Polyneices

3. How did the two brothers die?
   The two were on opposite sides in the recent civil war; they killed each other on the battlefield.

4. What is King Creon's decree?
   Polyneices was considered a traitor by King Creon for attacking the city of Thebes. Polyneices body was not permitted to be buried, but left for the scavenger birds and dogs to eat. Eteocles was to receive a hero's burial.

5. What does Antigone plan to do?
   She plans to bury her brother Polyneices according to the laws of their God. She believes that God's laws are more important than man's laws.

6. What is Ismene's decision regarding the King's decree?
   She is too afraid of recrimination to help Antigone.

7. What does the Choragos compare Polyneices to in the Parodos?
   He is compared to a wild eagle swooping down on the city of Thebes.

8. What city has "seven gates in a yawning ring"?
   The city of Thebes.

9. What does the Chorus compare Thebes to?
   Thebes, in this case, is the personification of those who rise to defend the city. Collectively, Thebes is compared to a dragon.

10. According to the Choragos, what does God hate?
    God hates "the bray of bragging tongues." He hates those who arrogantly brag of their successes.

Scene 1 and Ode 1:

1. Who is the new King of Thebes?
    Creon, brother-in-law to Oedipus, is the new king of Thebes.

2. How did the new King of Thebes claim heir to the throne?
    Creon is the brother-in-law of the previous king, Oedipus. When Oedipus' two sons were killed in battle, Creon was the next male in line for the throne.

3. What crime has Ployneices committed in the opinion of the king?
    Since Polyneices broke his exile and attacked the city of Thebes, Creon considers Polyneices a traitor.

4. What news does the sentry bring to Creon?
    Someone has secretly covered the body of Polyneices with just enough dirt to be considered as buried by the gods. His soul will now move to the Underworld.

5. How was it decided which of the sentries would bring the news about Polyneices to Creon?
    Since this is terribly bad news, no one wants to tell the king. The sentries end up throwing dice to decide who will tell Creon.

6. How does Creon believe the act of burying Polyneices was carried out?
    Creon believes that the sentries were paid off by his enemies and they were bribed to bury Polyneices' body.

7. What does Creon demand that the sentry do?
    King Creon demands that the sentry bring him the man who broke his decree and buried a traitor.

8. According to Ode 1, what is the most wonderful of all the world's wonders?
    Man is the most wonderful of all the world's wonders.

9. Of all the winds, man has made himself secure against all except one. Which wind is that?
    Man has not secured himself against the wind of death.

10. List man's accomplishments according to Ode 1.
    a. *He conquered the seas.*
    b. *He planted and harvested the Earth.*
    c. *He has command over the creatures of the earth (birds and fish as well).*
    d. *He has created language.*
    e. *He has built shelters against the elements.*
    f. *He has created government.*

Scene 2 and Ode 2:

1. Who has the sentry captured and brought before King Creon?
   The sentry brought Antigone, the king's niece, to Creon.

2. How did the guards manage to capture Antigone?
   The sentries had gone back to Polyneices' buried body and removed the dirt, thereby unburying it. They then sat back to watch who would come to bury it again.

3. How did Antigone react to being captured by the sentries?
   Antigone did not resist, but went with the sentries willingly.

4. What reason does Antigone give for defying Creon's decree?
   Antigone believes that the laws of God concerning the burial of the dead are more important than any of man's laws, including Creon's.

5. Who else does Creon have arrested in connection with the crime of burying Polyneices?
   He arrests Antigone's sister, Ismene in connection with the crime.

6. Why is Antigone angry with Ismene?
   Ismene wants to share in Antigone's guilt and punishment for burying Polyneices, yet she had refused to help her sister bury their brother.

7. Besides being Antigone's uncle, how else were Creon and Antigone related?
   Antigone was engaged to marry Creon's son, Haimon.

8. What is to be Antigone's punishment for burying her brother?
   Antigone will be put to death.

9. According to Ode 2, who is the fortunate man?
   The fortunate man is one "who has never tasted God's vengeance."

10. Who is the god who must not be made angry, according to Ode 2?
    Zeus must not be made angry or those who do will suffer his wrath.

Scene 3 and Ode 3:

1. What is Haimon's initial response when his father asks how he feels about the king's decision to execute Antigone?
   Haimon says that he supports and obeys his father's decisions.

2. What does Creon say that men pray for?
   Creon says that men pray for sons who are attentive and dutiful to their fathers.

3. Why is Creon intent on harshly punishing, even family members, all those who break the law?
   Creon believes that his people will not obey or have respect for him if he is lenient with family members.

4. What does Haimon claim is God's crowning gift to man?
   Haimon claims that the ability to reason is God's crowning gift to man.

5. What does Haimon tell King Creon about the people of Thebes' allegiance to him?
   Haimon tells his father that the people only obey him out of fear and that they will say whatever he wants to hear.

6. Whose point, King Creon's or Haimon's, does the Choragos support?
   The Choragos claims that both speak well. It is an effort to seek compromise.

7. How does the city feel about Antigone's crime?
   Haimon claims that the city of Thebes does not view Antigone as a criminal.

8. While Creon is ranting at his son, what does the king threaten to do?
   Creon threatens to execute Antigone, Haimon's fiancée, in front of him.

9. Describe Creon's death sentence for Antigone.
   Creon will have Antigone locked in a stone vault out in the wilderness. She will be given some provisions of food, and if she is able to escape, then it will be because her gods took pity on her.

10. According to Ode 3, what is it that "even the pure Immortals cannot escape"?
    "Even the pure Immortals cannot escape" love.

Scene 4 and Ode 4:
1. Whose fate does Antigone compare to her own?
   Antigone compares her fate to that of Niobe, Tantalos' daughter.

2. What does Antigone beg the people of Thebes to bear witness to?
   She wants the town to bear witness to how she was denied pity and unjustly judged by Creon.

3. Who does Antigone blame for her terrible misfortune?
   She blames the sins of her father, Oedipus for her misfortune.

4. According to the chorus, what is considered a virtue?
   Reverence to the gods is considered a virtue.

5. What does Creon sarcastically say would have man singing forever?
   Creon claims that if the singing of dirges and planned lamentations could put off death, men would sing forever.

6. According to Ode 4, who was locked away in a brazen vault?
   Danae was locked in a brazen vault.

7. Who came to the princess while she was locked away?
   Zeus came to Danae in her vault in the form of golden rain.

8. Who "bore the gods' prisoning anger for his pride"?
   Dryas' son

9. What is the "half remembered tale of horror" that old men tell?
   A king's new woman, sick with hatred for the queen he had imprisoned, ripped out his two sons' eyes with her bloody hands.

10. Who, as a child, had "raced with young colts on the glittering hills/And walked untrammeled in open light"?
    The daughter of the god of the North Wind was that child. She was also the mother of the two blinded boys.

Scene 5:

1. Who is the blind prophet who comes to speak to King Creon?
   Teiresias is the blind prophet.

2. What does the prophet claim that he heard which frightened him?
   He heard birds screaming and he knew that they were fighting and tearing at each other.

3. What happened when the prophet began "the rites of burnt-offering at the altar"?
   Although Teiresias claimed that Hephaistos failed him because he could not start a fire on the altar, the fat from the animal's thigh melted, the entrails dissolved, and bare bones burst forth from the body.

4. What does the prophet claim to be the cause of the gods' reaction to their offerings?
   Creon has brought about the anger of the gods with his decree about Polyneices and now the animals offered for sacrifice are the same animals that have been eating of Polyneices' body in the field. Because of this, the animals are unclean and not fit for sacrifice.

5. What does the prophet claim can be done to repair the evil performed against the gods?
   Creon is told that he can admit he was wrong and that he can make amends to the gods by burying Polyneices and by releasing Antigone.

6. What is King Creon's reaction to Teiresias' message?
   Creon becomes angry with Teiresias and refuses to yield.

7. What is it that Creon claims all prophets love?
   Creon claims that all prophets love gold.

8. What warning does Teiresias give to King Creon if he refuses to heed the prophesies?
   Teiresias warns Creon that he shall have to "pay back/Corpse for corpse, flesh of [his] own flesh" as punishment for angering the gods.

9. What advice does the Choragos give King Creon once Teiresias leaves?
   The Choragos advises Creon to quickly "free Antigone from the vault/ And build a tomb for Polyneices" in order to appease the gods' anger.

10. How does King Creon react to the advice of the Choragos?
    Creon finally admits to his pride and says that he himself will go to set Antigone free.

Paean and Exodos:
1. The Choragos and the Chorus pray to a "God of many names." What are some of these names?
   a. *Iacchos, son of Kadmeian Semele*
   b. *Born of the Thunder*
   c. *Guardian of the West Regent of Eleusis' plain*
   d. *Prince of Maenad Thebes and the Dragon Field*
   e. *Heavenly Child of Semele Bride of Thunderer*
   f. *Io Iacche*

2. Who does the messenger claim is "a walking dead man"?
   King Creon is a walking dead man.

3. How has Teiresias' prophecy that Creon would pay to the gods "flesh of [his] own flesh" come true?
   The messenger reports that Haimon, Creon's son, has killed himself.

4. Who is Eurydice?
   She is Creon's wife and the mother of Haimon.

5. What were Creon and the messenger doing when they prayed to Hecate and Pluto?
   Creon and the messenger were bathing the corpse of Polyneices with holy water before they burned what was left of it. They then "heaped up a towering barrow/Of earth of his own land" over the urn.

6. What did King Creon and the messenger do as soon as they finished their tasks regarding Polyneices?
   They hurried to the vault to set Antigone free.

7. Describe what Creon saw when he looked through the crevice into Antigone's tomb.
   Creon saw Haimon weeping over Antigone's dead body. She had hanged herself with her own veil. Haimon was holding her body close to him and crying that "his father had stolen her away from him".

8. Describe Haimon's reaction when Creon entered Antigone's tomb.
   Haimon spat in his father's face and then he drew his sword against Creon. When he missed in his attempt to kill the king, he turned the sword on himself. He died with Antigone in his arms.

9. What happened after the messenger relayed the news about Haimon and Antigone to Eurydice?
   Eurydice walked silently into the house, went to the altar and killed herself.

10. What does the Choragos claim is "always punished" by the gods?
    The gods always punish "big words" (pride).

STUDY GUIDE/QUIZ QUESTIONS - *Antigone*
Multiple Choice Format

Prologue and Parodos:

1. How are Antigone and Ismene related?
    A. They are cousins.
    B. Antigone is Ismene's daughter.
    C. They are sisters.
    D. Ismene is Antigone's daughter.

2. Who are the two brothers mentioned in the prologue?
    A. Oedipus and Creon
    B. Zeus and Dionysus
    C. Antigone and Ismene
    D. Eteocles and Polyneices

3. How did the two brothers die?
    A. They were executed for treason.
    B. They killed each other in battle.
    C. Antigone poisoned them.
    D. They were hanged for wounding a fellow officer.

4. What is King Creon's decree?
    A. Eteocles is to be buried with honors while Polyneices is left for the birds
    B. Polyneices is to be buried with honors while Eteocles is left for the birds.
    C. Oedipus is to be exiled from Thebes.
    D. Antigone must die for burying her brother, Eteocles.

5. What does Antigone plan to do?
    A. She plans to marry Eteocles.
    B. She plans to bury her brother, Polyneices, secretly.
    C. She plans to bury her brother, Eteocles, secretly.
    D. She plans to assassinate the king.

6. What is Ismene's decision regarding the King's decree?
    A. She agrees with Antigone and they bury Eteocles.
    B. She is afraid to go against the king, so she refuses to help her sister.
    C. She agrees with Antigone and they bury Polyneices.
    D. She plans to tell the king about Antigone's decision.

7. What does the Choragos compare Polyneices to in the Parodos?
    A. a dragon
    B. a lion
    C. a bull
    D. a wild eagle

Antigone Multiple Choice Study/Quiz Questions
Prologue and Parodos Multiple Choice Continued

8. What city has "seven gates in a yawning ring"?
    A. Athens
    B. Thebes
    C. Ithaca
    D. Ismarus

9. What does the Chorus compare Thebes to?
    A. a dragon
    B. a lion
    C. a bull
    D. a wild eagle

10. According to the Choragos, what does God hate?
    A. a liar
    B. a murderer
    C. a braggart
    D. a thief

Antigone Multiple Choice Study/Quiz Questions

Scene 1 and Ode 1:
1. Who is the new King of Thebes?
    A. Polyneices
    B. Eteocles
    C. Oedipus
    D. Creon

2. How did the new King of Thebes claim heir to the throne?
    A. The former king was his father.
    B. The former king was his brother-in-law whose sons both died in battle.
    C. The former king was his uncle.
    D. The former king left no heir, so Creon simply took the empty throne.

3. What crime has Ployneices committed in the opinion of the king?
    A. murder
    B. treason
    C. theft
    D. adultery

4. What news does the sentry bring to Creon?
    A. Polyneices is dead
    B. The people of Thebes are preparing to riot because of the king's decree.
    C. Someone has gone against the king's decree and buried Polynieces.
    D. Someone has removed the body of Polyneices from the field where it had been left.

5. How was it decided which of the sentries would bring the news about Polyneices to Creon?
    A. They drew straws.
    B. They did rock, paper, scissors.
    C. They drew slips of paper; the one with the black spot had to tell the king.
    D. They tossed dice.

6. How does Creon believe the act of burying Polyneices was carried out?
    A. The king's known political enemies crept onto the field at night.
    B. One of the guards must have moved the body and handed it over to the priests.
    C. Polyneices' wife paid the sentries to allow her to bury her husband.
    D. The sentries had been bribed by the king's enemies, and they buried the body.

7. What does Creon demand that the sentry do?
    A. find the man who defied his order and bring him to the king
    B. uncover the body so that it's soul cannot go to the Underworld
    C. burn the body
    D. kill the traitors who defied his order

Antigone Multiple Choice Study/Quiz Questions
Scene 1 and Ode 1 Continued

8. According to Ode 1, what is the most wonderful of all the world's wonders?
    A. the storm gray sea
    B. man
    C. the lightbones birds and beasts
    D. the lion on a hill

9. Of all the winds, man has made himself secure against all except one. Which wind is that?
    A. the mighty North wind
    B. the sultry South wind
    C. the wind of Death
    D. the dry West wind

10. Which of the following is not one of man's accomplishments according to Ode 1?
    A. He has created government.
    B. He has conquered the seas.
    C. He has created roads to reach far lands.
    D. He has created language.

Antigone Multiple Choice Study/Quiz Questions

Scene 2 and Ode 2:
1. Who has the sentry captured and brought before King Creon?
    A. Polyneices
    B. Antigone
    C. Ismene
    D. Eteocles

2. How did the guards manage to capture Antigone?
    A. They removed the dirt from Polyneices' body and waited to see who came back.
    B. Ismene told the sentries where to find her.
    C. When she was going back to the body, she tripped, making a large noise.
    D. They didn't capture her; she turned herself in.

3. How did Antigone react to being taken by the sentries?
    A. She bit the sentry who was delivering her to Creon.
    B. She begged them to let her go because she was merely burying her brother.
    C. She went with them freely and without a fuss.
    D. She tried to run, but she was caught and tied up.

4. What reason does Antigone give for defying Creon's decree?
    A. She had not heard the decree.
    B. She was trying to get back at Creon for taking the crown of Thebes.
    C. Ismene forced her to do it against her will.
    D. God's laws demand burial, and they are more important than man's laws.

5. Who else does Creon have arrested in connection with the crime of burying Polyneices?
    A. Eteocles
    B. Ismene
    C. the sentry
    D. Oedipus

6. Why is Antigone angry with Ismene?
    A. Ismene planned to share in Antigone's punishment, but would not help her.
    B. Ismene told the sentries that Antigone had buried Polyneices
    C. Ismene told Creon what Antigone had planned.
    D. Ismene refuses to acknowledge Antigone as her sister.

7. Besides being Antigone's uncle, how else are Creon and Antigone related?
    A. They are cousins.
    B. Antigone is the mother of his child.
    C. Creon and Antigone are both siblings to Oedipus.
    D. Antigone is engaged to Creon's son.

Antigone Multiple Choice Study/Quiz Questions
Scene 2 and Ode 2 Continued

8. What is to be Antigone's punishment for burying her brother?
    A. She will be publicly whipped.
    B. She will be banished from Thebes forever.
    C. She will die.
    D. She will be chained to a rock for a terrible monster to find and destroy her.

9. According to Ode 2, who is the fortunate man?
    A. one who has found true love
    B. one who has never tasted God's vengeance
    C. one who has learned compassion for others
    D. one who has learned to reason

10. Who is the god who must not be made angry, according to Ode 2?
    A. Dionysus
    B. Poseidon
    C. Zeus
    D. Hades

Anigone Multiple Choice Study/Quiz Questions

Scene 3 and Ode 3:

1. What is Haimon's initial response when his father asks how he feels about the king's decision to execute Antigone?
    - A. He is outraged that his father would execute his own niece.
    - B. He falls to he knees and begs his father to kill him in her place.
    - C. He tells his father that he supports and obeys his father's decisions.
    - D. He agrees that Antigone should be executed for her crime against the state.

2. What does Creon say that men pray for?
    - A. loyal wives
    - B. dutiful sons
    - C. subordinates who follow orders unquestioningly
    - D. the strength to do what is right and pleasing in God's eyes

3. Which of the following is not one of the reasons why Creon is intent on harshly punishing, even family members, all those who break the law?
    - A. He believes that his people will not respect him as king if he shows leniency.
    - B. He is afraid of appearing weak in the eyes of his people.
    - C. He wants to make an example of Antigone to demonstrate his power.
    - D. He is an envious man who would never relinquish the throne under any circumstances.

4. What does Haimon claim is God's crowning gift to man?
    - A. the love of a good woman
    - B. the ability to reason
    - C. his power over the creatures of the Earth
    - D. the ability to be compassionate

5. What does Haimon tell King Creon about the people of Thebes' allegiance to him?
    - A. He says that they are willing to defend him from any opponents.
    - B. He says that the people have no respect for Creon and ridicule him behind his back.
    - C. He says that the people only follow Creon out of fear and say what Creon wants to hear.
    - D. He says that the people are prepared to revolt if Creon does not free Antigone.

6. Whose point, King Creon's or Haimon's, does the Choragos support?
    - A. King Creaon's
    - B. Haimon's
    - C. He says that both positions have merit.
    - D. He says that they are both fools.

Antigone Multiple Choice Study/Quiz Questions
Scene 3 and Ode 3

7. How does the city feel about Antigone's crime?
    A. They do not view it as a crime, but as a loving sister caring for her dead brother.
    B. They want Creon to execute her publicly.
    C. They believe that Antigone's body should suffer that same fate decreed to Polyneices'.
    D. They believe that Antigone should be merely banished and not executed.

8. While Creon is ranting at his son, what does the king threaten to do?
    A. He threatens to kill Haimon.
    B. He threatens to kill Antigone right in front of Haimon's eyes.
    C. He threatens to banish Haimon for going against him.
    D. He threatens to disinherit Haimon so that Haimon could never become king.

9. Describe Creon's death sentence for Antigone.
    A. She will be hanged by the neck until dead.
    B. She will be shot at dawn.
    C. She will be locked in a stone tomb with only enough food for one day and left to die.
    D. She will be publicly stoned to death.

10. According to Ode 3, what is it that "even the pure Immortals cannot escape"?
    A. death
    B. love
    C. reason
    D. betrayal

Antigone Multiple Choice/Quiz Questions

Scene 4 and Ode 4:
1. Whose fate does Antigone compare to her own?
    A. Polyneices
    B. Niobe
    C. Eteocles
    D. Oedipus

2. What does Antigone beg the people of Thebes to bear witness to?
    A. her curse against Creon
    B. his reverence for the gods
    C. her love for Haimon
    D. how she was denied pity and unjustly judged

3. Who does Antigone blame for her terrible misfortune?
    A. Creon
    B. Polyneices
    C. Oedipus
    D. Haimon

4. According to the chorus, what is considered a virtue?
    A. reverence
    B. humility
    C. silence
    D. trustworthiness

5. What does Creon sarcastically say would have man singing forever?
    A. lewd women
    B. their own pride
    C. their greed
    D. if death could be postponed by singing

6. According to Ode 4, who was locked away in a brazen vault?
    A. Antigone
    B. Danae
    C. Oedipus
    D. Polyneices

7. Who came to the princess while she was locked away?
    A. Pluto
    B. Creon
    C. Zeus
    D. Hephaestus

Antigone Multiple Choice Study/Quiz Questions

Scene 4 and Ode 4

8. Who "bore the gods' prisoning anger for his pride"?
   A. Creon
   B. Dryas' son
   C. Zeus
   D. Polyneices

9. What is the "half remembered tale of horror" that old men tell?
   A. A young girl is chained to a rock to await a terrible monster.
   B. A man was wandering in a labyrinth to seek out the Minotaur.
   C. A king's mistress tore out the eyes of his sons in a jealous rage.
   D. Young men gazed at Medusa and were instantly turned to stone.

10. Who, as a child, had "raced with young colts on the glittering hills/And walked untrammeled in open light"?
    A. Antigone
    B. Creon
    C. Oedipus
    D. the daughter of the god of the North Wind

Antigone Multiple Choice Study/Quiz Questions

Scene 5:
1. Who is the blind prophet who comes to speak to King Creon?
    A. Oedipus
    B. Eurydice
    C. Choragos
    D. Teiresias

2. What does the prophet claim that he heard which frightened him?
    A. birds screeching and fighting
    B. a lion roar
    C. thunder
    D. the voice of Zeus condemning Creon

3. What happened when the prophet began "the rites of burnt-offering at the altar"?
    A. The flames instantly turned all to white ash.
    B. The animal's body exploded in Teiresias' face.
    C. There was no flame, but the sacrifice melted on the altar.
    D. The gods accepted the offering.

4. What does the prophet claim to be the cause of the gods' reaction to their offerings?
    A. They are angry that Antigone defied Creon.
    B. They are angry that Creon refuses to pay homage to the gods in any way.
    C. They are angry regarding Creaon's treatment of Polyneices.
    D. Antigone must pay for the sins of her father, Oedipus.

5. What does the prophet claim can be done to repair the evil performed against the gods?
    A. Antigone should beg mercy of Creon.
    B. Creon should admit his errors and put them right.
    C. Creon can offer a sacrifice on the altar of Zeus to atone for his sins.
    D. Antigone can publicly apologize for defying Creon's decree.

6. What is King Creon's reaction to Teiresias' message?
    A. He angrily refuses to yield because he does not want to appear weak.
    B. He believes that Teiresias is lying to him and that he is no prophet.
    C. He is glad that the gods will relent if Antigone apologizes.
    D. He repents his errors and tries to make amends.

7. What is it that Creon claims all prophets love?
    A. gold
    B. power
    C. fame
    D. wisdom

Antigone Multiple Choice Study/Quiz Questions
Scene 5

8. What warning does Teiresias give to King Creon if he refuses to heed the prophesies?
    A. Creon will die.
    B. the king will lose what is dear to him in repayment to the gods.
    C. Antigone will haunt his dreams forever.
    D. the city of Thebes will rise against him and revolt.

9. What advice does the Choragos give King Creon once Teiresias leaves?
    A. to make a sacrifice to Zeus
    B. to ignore the ramblings of a crazy old man
    C. to heed the warning by freeing Antigone and building a tomb for Polyneices
    D. to arrest Teiresias as a traitor

10. How does King Creon react to the advice of the Choragos?
    A. He refuses to make a sacrifice to the gods.
    B. He sacrifices a dove to Zeus as a peace offering.
    C. He has Teiresias arrested and tried for treason.
    D. He hurries to release Antigone and bury Polyneices.

Antigone Multiple Choice Study/Quiz Questions

Paean and Exodos:
1. The Choragos and the Chorus pray to a "God of many names". Which of the following is not one of these names?
    A. Guardian of the West Regent of Eleusis' plain
    B. Io Iacche
    C. god of the North Wind
    D. Prince of the Dragon Field

2. Who does the messenger claim is "a walking dead man"?
    A. Polyneices
    B. Creon
    C. Teiresias
    D. Oedipus

3. How has Teiresias' prophecy that Creon would pay to the gods "flesh of [his] own flesh" come true?
    A. Creon was forced to yield a pound of flesh as a burnt-offering.
    B. Creon's only daughter was struck down by the gods in vengeance for Antigone.
    C. Creon's son has killed himself.
    D. Creon's lineage is cursed by the gods for twenty generations.

4. Who is Eurydice?
    A. Creon's wife
    B. Antigone's sister
    C. Creon's only daughter
    D. Antigone's mother

5. What were Creon and the messenger doing when they prayed to Hecate and Pluto?
    A. begging the gods to remove the curse from Creon's family
    B. burying Polyneices
    C. freeing Antigone
    D. praying to restore Polyneices to life

6. What did King Creon and the messenger do as soon as they finished their tasks regarding Polyneices?
    A. went to free Antigone
    B. sacrificed a pure white goat to Pluto in thanks
    C. sacrificed a young bull to Zeus to beg forgiveness
    D. returned to Thebes

Antigone Multiple Choice Study/Quiz Questions
Scene 5

7. Describe what Creon saw when he looked through the crevice into Antigone's tomb.
   A. Antigone's body was hanging from the ceiling by her own veil.
   B. Haimon was weeping over the dead body of Antigone.
   C. Haimon was rescuing Antigone from the tomb; they were running away.
   D. Antigone was praying to the gods for help.

8. Describe Haimon's reaction when Creon entered Antigone's tomb.
   A. He put Antigone's dead body at Creon's feet.
   B. He ran in fear of being accused of treason.
   C. He attacked Creon.
   D. He wept in his father's arms.

9. What happened after the messenger relayed the news about Haimon and Antigone to Eurydice?
   A. She made a sacrifice of thanks to Zeus.
   B. She killed Creon.
   C. She rejoiced that Haimon and Antigone were finally together.
   D. She killed herself.

10. What does the Choragos claim is "always punished" by the gods?
    A. greed
    B. lust
    C. big words
    D. treason

ANSWER KEY - MULTIPLE CHOICE STUDY/QUIZ QUESTIONS - *Antigone*

Prologue/Parodos	Scene 1/Ode 1	Scene 2/Ode 2	Scene 3/Ode 3
1. C	1. D	1. B	1. C
2. D	2. B	2. A	2. B
3. B	3. B	3. C	3. D
4. A	4. C	4. D	4. B
5. B	5. D	5. B	5. C
6. B	6. D	6. A	6. C
7. D	7. A	7. D	7. A
8. B	8. B	8. C	8. B
9. A	9. C	9. B	9. C
10. C	10. C	10. C	10. B

Scene 4/Ode 4	Scene 5	Paean and Exodos
1. B	1. D	1. C
2. D	2. A	2. B
3. C	3. C	3. C
4. A	4. C	4. A
5. D	5. B	5. B
6. B	6. A	6. A
7. C	7. A	7. B
8. B	8. B	8. C
9. C	9. C	9. D
10. D	10. D	10. C

PREREADING VOCABULARY WORKSHEETS

VOCABULARY FOR THE PROLOGUE AND PARADOS - *Antigone*

Part I: Using Prior Knowledge and Contextual Clues

Below are the sentences in which the vocabulary words appear in the text. Read the sentence. Use any clues you can find in the sentence combined with your prior knowledge, and write what you think the underlined words mean on the lines provided.

1. "Have they told you of the new ***decree*** of our King Creon?"

   _____

2. "No one shall bury him, no one mourn for him,/But his body must lie in the fields, a sweet treasure/For ***carrion*** birds to find as they search for food."

   _____

3. "I beg the Dead/To forgive me, but I am helpless; I must ***yield***/To those in authority."

   _____

4. "You need not be [afraid];/You have yourself to ***consider***, after all."

   _____

5. "Polyneices their commander/***Roused*** them with windy phrases,/He the wild eagle screaming/Insults above our land . . ."

   _____

6. "O marching light/Across the ***eddy*** and rush of Dirce's stream . . ."

   _____

7. ". . . His wings their shields of snow,/His crest their ***marshal***ed helms."

   _____

8. "The famished spears came onward in the night;/But before his jaws were ***sated*** with our blood, . . . /His power was thrown back. . ."

   _____

9. "For God hates utterly/The ***bray*** of bragging tongues . . ."

   _____

Antigone Vocabulary Prologue and Parados

10. ". . . And when he beheld their smiling,/Their **_swagger_** of golden helms,/the frown of his thunder blasted/Their first man from our walls."

_____

Part II: Determining the Meaning
   Match the vocabulary words to their dictionary definitions

   ___ 1. decree   A. To think carefully about
   ___ 2. carrion   B. To satisfy to excess
   ___ 3. yield   C. A current of water moving against the direction of the main current
   ___ 4. consider   D. A loud, harsh sound resembling that of a donkey
   ___ 5. roused   E. feeding on dead and decaying flesh.
   ___ 6. eddy   F. A military officer of the highest rank in some countries
   ___ 7. marshal   G. An authoritative order having the force of law
   ___ 8. sated   H. To excite, as to anger or action; stir up
   ___ 9. bray   I. To walk or conduct oneself with an insolent or arrogant air; strut
   ___ 10. swagger   J. To give up (an advantage, for example) to another; concede.

VOCABULARY FOR SCENE ONE AND ODE ONE - *Antigone*

Part I: Using Prior Knowledge and Contextual Clues

Below are the sentences in which the vocabulary words appear in the text. Read the sentence. Use any clues you can find in the sentence combined with your prior knowledge, and write what you think the underlined words mean on the lines provided.

1. "In this ***auspicious*** dawn of his reign/What are the new complexities/That shifting Fate has woven for him?"

   _____

2. ". . . I say to you at the very outset that I have nothing but ***contempt*** for the kind of Governor who is afraid, for whatever reason, to follow the course that he knows is best for the State. . . "

   _____

3. "I do not mean that; the ***sentries*** have been appointed."

   _____

4. "A ***comprehensive*** defense! More effective, perhaps,/If I knew its purpose."

   _____

5. "There have been those who have whispered together,/Stiff-necked ***anarchists***, putting their heads together,/Scheming against me in alleys."

   _____

6. "There's nothing in the world so ***demoralizing*** as money."

   _____

7. ". . . the stormgray sea/Yields to his ***prow***, the huge crests bear him high . . . "

   _____

8. "The lightboned birds and beasts that cling to cover,/The ***lithe*** fish lighting their reaches of dim water,/All are taken, tamed in the net of his mind . . ."

   _____

9. ". . . his blunt yoke has broken/The ***sultry*** shoulders of the mountain bull."

   _____

Antigone Vocabulary Worksheet Scene 1 and Ode 1 Continued

10. "And his the skill that ***deflects*** the arrows of snow,/The spears of winter rain . . ."

___

Part II: Determining the Meaning
  Match the vocabulary words to their dictionary definitions

____ 1. auspicious   A. very humid and hot
____ 2. contempt   B. attended by favorable circumstances
____ 3. sentries   C. to undermine the confidence or morale of; dishearten
____ 4. comprehensive   D. the feeling or attitude of regarding someone or something as
                               inferior
____ 5. anarchists   E. marked by or showing extensive understanding
____ 6. demoralizing   F. turns aside or cause to turn aside
____ 7. prow   G. those who reject of all forms of coercive control and authority
____ 8. lithe   H. soldiers posted to prevent the passage of unauthorized persons
____ 9. sultry   I. the forward part of a ship's hull
____ 10. deflects   J. marked by effortless grace

VOCABULARY FOR SCENE TWO AND ODE TWO - *Antigone*

Part I: Using Prior Knowledge and Contextual Clues

Below are the sentences in which the vocabulary words appear in the text. Read the sentence. Use any clues you can find in the sentence combined with your prior knowledge, and write what you think the underlined words mean on the lines provided.

1. "A storm of dust roared up from the earth, and the sky/Went out, the plain vanished with all its trees/In the stinging dark. We closed our eyes and ***endured*** it."

   _____

2. "Tell me, tell me briefly;/Had you heard my ***proclamation*** touching this matter?"

   _____

3. "And yet you dared ***defy*** the law."

   _____

4. "Your ***edict***, King, was strong,/But all your strength is weakness itself against/The immortal unrecorded laws of God."

   _____

5. "This girl is guilty of a double ***insolence***,/Breaking the given laws and boasting of it."

   _____

6. ". . . generation from generation/Takes the ***compulsive*** rage of the enemy god."

   _____

7. "What mortal arrogance/***Transcends*** the wrath of Zeus?"

   _____

8. "The straying dreams of men/May bring them ghosts of joy;/ . . . as they ***drowse*** . . ."

   _____

9. ". . . the waking ***embers*** burn them;/Or they walk with fixed eyes, as blind men walk."

   _____

Antigone Vocabulary Worksheet Scene 2 and Ode 2 Continued

10. Fortunate is the man who has never tasted God's ***vengeance***!"

_____

Part II: Determining the Meaning
  Match the vocabulary words to their dictionary definitions

___ 1. endured   A. infliction of punishment in return for a wrong committed
___ 2. proclamation   B. a formal command
___ 3. defy   C. to pass beyond the limits of something
___ 4. edict   D. rudeness or disrespect
___ 5. insolence   E. bore with tolerance
___ 6. compulsive   F. to refuse to submit to or cooperate with
___ 7. transcends   G. having the capacity to exert a strong, irresistible force on
___ 8. drowse   H. a small, glowing piece of coal or wood, as in a dying fire
___ 9. embers   I. to be half-asleep
___ 10. vengeance   J. an official formal public announcement

VOCABULARY FOR SCENE THREE AND ODE THREE - *Antigone*

Part I: Using Prior Knowledge and Contextual Clues

Below are the sentences in which the vocabulary words appear in the text. Read the sentence. Use any clues you can find in the sentence combined with your prior knowledge, and write what you think the underlined words mean on the lines provided.

1. "We shall soon see, and no need of ***diviners***."

   _____

2. "Have you come here hating me, or have you come/With ***deference*** and with love, whatever I do?"

   _____

3. "That is the way to behave; ***subordinate***/Everything else, my son, to your father's will."

   _____

4. ". . . But since we are all too likely to go ***astray*** ,/The reasonable thing is to learn from those who can teach."

   _____

5. "So? Your 'concern'? In a public ***brawl*** with your father!"

   _____

6. "If you were not my father,/I'd say you were ***perverse***."

   _____

7. ". . . she may learn, though late,/that ***piety*** shown the dead is pity in vain."

   _____

8. "Love, unconquerable/Waster of rich men, keeper/Of warm lights and all night ***vigil*** . . ."

   _____

9. "You'll never see me taken in by anything so ***vile***."

   _____

Antigone Vocabulary Worksheet Scene 3 and Ode 3 Continued

10. "...the same thing happens in sailing;/Make your sheet fast, never ***slacken***—and over you go."

_____

Part II: Determining the Meaning
  Match the vocabulary words to their dictionary definitions

  ___ 1. diviners   A. to subject to the authority or control of another
  ___ 2. deference   B. righteousness by virtue of being pious
  ___ 3. subordinate   C. to make or become less tense, taut, or firm; loosen
  ___ 4. astray   D. deserving of contempt or scorn
  ___ 5. brawl   E. a watch kept during normal sleeping hours
  ___ 6. perverse   F. straying to or into wrong or evil ways
  ___ 7. piety   G. yielding to the opinion, wishes, or judgment of another
  ___ 8. vigil   H. those who can predict the future; fortune-tellers
  ___ 9. vile   I. obstinately persisting in an error; wrongly self-willed or stubborn
  ___ 10. slacken   J. a noisy quarrel or fight

VOCABULARY FOR SCENE 4 AND ODE 4 - *Antigone*

Part I: Using Prior Knowledge and Contextual Clues

Below are the sentences in which the vocabulary words appear in the text. Read the sentence. Use any clues you can find in the sentence combined with your prior knowledge, and write what you think the underlined words mean on the lines provided.

1. "How often have I heard the story of Niobe,/Tantalos' **wretched** daughter, how the stone/Clung fast about her, ivy-close . . ."

   _____

2. "I have been a stranger here in my own land:/All my life/The **blasphemy** of my birth has followed me."

   _____

3. "Lead me to my vigil, where I must have/Neither love nor **lamentation**, no song, but silence."

   _____

4. "If **dirges** and planned lamentations could put off death,/Men would be singing forever."

   _____

5. "O passionate heart,/Unyielding, **tormented** still by the same winds!"

   _____

6. "You will remember/What things I suffer, and at what men's hands,/Because I would not **transgress** the laws of heaven."

   _____

7. "All Danae's beauty was locked away/In a **brazen** cell where the sunlight could not come . . ."

   _____

8. "No power in wealth or war/Or tough sea-blackened ships/Can **prevail** against untiring Destiny!"

   _____

Antigone Vocabulary Worksheet Scene 4 and Ode 4 Continued

9. "... he had profaned the revels,/And fired the wrath of the nine/***Implacable*** Sisters that love the sound of the flute."

_____

10. "Her father was the god of the North Wind/And she was cradled by ***gales***..."

_____

Part II: Determining the Meaning
   Match the vocabulary words to their dictionary definitions

   ___ 1. wretched   A. a cry of sorrow and grief
   ___ 2. blasphemy   B. made of brass
   ___ 3. lamentation   C. caused great physical pain or mental anguish
   ___ 4. dirges   D. very strong winds
   ___ 5. tormented   E. impossible to placate or appease
   ___ 6. transgress   F. a profane act, utterance, or writing concerning God
   ___ 7. brazen   G. funeral hymns
   ___ 8. prevail   H. to be greater in strength or influence; triumph
   ___ 9. implacable   I. to commit an offense by violating a law or command; sin
   ___ 10. gales   J. in a deplorable state of distress or misfortune; miserable

VOCABULARY FOR SCENE 5, PAEAN AND EXODOS - *Antigone*

Part I: Using Prior Knowledge and Contextual Clues

Below are the sentences in which the vocabulary words appear in the text. Read the sentence. Use any clues you can find in the sentence combined with your prior knowledge, and write what you think the underlined words mean on the lines provided.

1. "Listen, Creon:/I was sitting in my chair of **_augury_**, at the place/Where the birds gather around me."

   _____

2. ". . . instead of bright flame,/There was only the sputtering slime of the fat thigh-flesh/Melting; the **_entrails_** dissolved in gray smoke . . ."

   _____

3. "I tell you, Creon, you yourself have brought/This new **_calamity_** upon us."

   _____

4. "Our hearths and altars/Are stained with the corruption of dogs and carrion birds/That **_glut_** themselves on the corpse of Oedipus' son."

   _____

5. "To do what? –Come let's have the **_aphorism_**!"

   _____

6. "God moves/Swiftly to cancel the **_folly_** of stubborn men."

   _____

7. "The shadow of plague is upon us:/come with **_clement_** feet/oh come from Parnasos/down the long slopes/across the lamenting water."

   _____

8. "Men of the line of Kadmos, you who live/Near Amphion's **_citadel_**; I cannot say/Of any condition of human life, 'This is fixed,/This is clearly good, or bad'."

   _____

Antigone Vocabulary Worksheet Scene 5, Paean and Exodos Continued

9. "Surely a god/Has crushed me beneath the hugest weight of heaven,/And driven me headlong in a ***barbaric*** way/To trample out the thing I held most dear."

_____

10. "And we bathed/The corpse with holy water, and we brought/Fresh-broken branches to burn what was left of it,/And upon the urn we heaped up a towering ***barrow*** of earth of his own land."

_____

Part II: Determining the Meaning
   Match the vocabulary words to their dictionary definitions

   ___ 1. augury   A. inclined to be lenient or merciful
   ___ 2. entrails   B. an event that brings terrible loss; disaster
   ___ 3. calamity   C. the internal organs, especially the intestines
   ___ 4. glut   D. a tersely phrased statement of a truth or opinion; an adage
   ___ 5. aphorism   E. a large mound of earth or stones placed over a burial site
   ___ 6. folly   F. the art, ability, or practice of divination or predictions
   ___ 7. clement   G. without civilizing influences
   ___ 8. citadel   H. a fortress in a commanding position in or near a city
   ___ 9. barbaric   I. to fill beyond capacity, especially with food
   ___ 10. barrow   J. a lack of good sense, understanding, or foresight

VOCABULARY ANSWER KEY - *Antigone*

<u>Prologue/Parodos</u>
1. G
2. E
3. J
4. A
5. H
6. C
7. F
8. B
9. D
10. I

<u>Scene 1/Ode 1</u>
1. B
2. D
3. H
4. E
5. G
6. C
7. I
8. J
9. A
10. F

<u>Scene 2/Ode 2</u>
1. E
2. J
3. F
4. B
5. D
6. G
7. C
8. I
9. H
10. A

<u>Scene 3/Ode 3</u>
1. H
2. G
3. A
4. F
5. J
6. I
7. B
8. E
9. D
10. C

<u>Scene 4/Ode 4</u>
1. J
2. F
3. A
4. G
5. C
6. I
7. B
8. H
9. E
10. D

<u>Scene 5, Paean and Exodos</u>
1. F
2. C
3. B
4. I
5. D
6. J
7. A
8. H
9. G
10. E

DAILY LESSONS

LESSON ONE

Objectives
- Students will become familiar with several Greek myths and be introduced to the elements of tragedy (from Aristotle's *Poetics*).
- Students will be briefly introduced to Sophocles' role as a playwright. (Other roles in his society will be part of a research project later on.)
- Students will be introduced to Sophocles' tragedy, *Antigone,* and the structure of a Greek Tragedy

Activity #1

Ask students to brainstorm what the term "tragedy" means, and try to come up with what elements of any plot could be considered as "tragic." Students share ideas aloud and write them on the chalk board. Ask students to brainstorm examples of tragedies from both literature and real life. List them on the board and discuss what makes each of these stories tragic. What do they all seem to have in common? Lead into discussion of the elements of a tragedy (see below).

The following list is compiled from Aristotle's *Poetics* and it contains the six main elements of a Tragedy:

I. **plot** – how the action is arranged
   A. *tragedy*: a play with a serious theme that usually ends unhappily for the main character set in motion by some tragic flaw in his/her personality (harmartia).
   B. *hubris*: arrogance demonstrated by a character as a result of his/her pride or passion
   C. *foreshadowing*: clues as to what will probably happen later in the play
   D. *climax*: the highest point of emotional tension or the turning point of the plot
   E. *catharsis*: the purification of a character's emotions and/or the relief of emotional tension
   F. *denouement*: the resolution of the main conflict (not usually a happy outcome for the main character)
II. **characters** – the people in the play
III. **theme** – the main idea or message as the central focus
IV. **language/diction** – the words spoken or sung by the characters
V. **music** – the odes sung by the chorus and choragus (in Greek tragedy)
VI. **spectacle** – the scenes, props, costumes, masks… anything visual

A Greek tragedy is structured as follows:

I. **Prologue:** Spoken by one or two characters before the chorus appears. The prologue usually gives the background information needed to understand the events of the play.
II. **Parodos:** the song sung by the chorus as it makes its entrance
III. **Episodes/Scenes:** the main action of the play
IV. **Odes:** songs (and often dance) that reflect on the events of the episodes, and weave the plot into a cohesive whole
   A. *Choragos:* the leader of the chorus who often interacts with the characters in the scenes.
   B. *Chorus:* the singers/dancers who remark on the action
      1. strophe: the movement of the chorus from right to left across the stage
      2. antistrophe: the reaction to the strophe, which moves across the stage from left to right.

V. **Paean:** a prayer of thanksgiving to Dionysos in whose honor the Greek plays were performed
VI. **Exodos:** sung by the chorus as it makes its final exit, which usually offers words of wisdom related to the actions and outcome of the play

Activity #2

Ask students to brainstorm any Greek myths that they are familiar with and write them on the board. (Try to lead students toward coming up with the tales listed below.) Have students talk together in partners to decide if any of the stories listed on the board would fit into the realm of a tragedy. Introduce each of the myths below and after briefly summarizing them (these tales can be easily found on the Internet as well as in any good book of mythology), write them as headings for columns on the front board. Based on the number of students in the classroom, create "slots" underneath each story for students to sign up for the one they would like to work on. (You could use a stack of 3x5 cards, one for each student, to shuffle and draw one by one at random and let the person on the card decide which story he/she wants. Once a category if filled, those whose cards are drawn later must fill in the missing slots.) Pass out the group writing assignment (see below). ***Three to four*** members per group is ideal.

Greek myths with tragic plots: (Feel free to add others.)
1. Cupid and Psyche
2. Pandora's box
3. Hercules (before he had to perform his twelve labors)
4. Narcissus
5. Echo
6. Callisto and Arcas
7. Atreus
8. Orpheus

Activity #3

Give brief notes about Sophocles' life and role as a playwright in Greek culture. (See the introductory materials for this LitPlan) Save the discussion of his other roles in Greek society for the students' research papers.

Activity #4

Distribute the materials students will use in this unit. Explain in detail how students are to use these materials.

Study Guides   Students should read the study guide questions for each reading assignment prior to beginning the reading assignment to get a feeling for what events and ideas are important in the section they are about to read. After reading the section, students will (as a class or individually) answer the questions to review the important events and ideas from that section of the play. Students should keep the study guides as study materials for the unit test.

Vocabulary   Prior to each reading assignment, students will do vocabulary work related to the section of the work they are about to read. Following the completion of the reading of the play, there will be a vocabulary review of all the words used in the vocabulary assignments. Students should keep their vocabulary work as study materials for the unit test.

<u>Reading Assignment Sheet</u>   You need to fill in the reading assignment sheet to let students know by when their reading has to be completed. You can either write the assignment sheet up on a side blackboard or bulletin board and leave it there for students to see each day, or you can photocopy schedules for each student to have. In either case, you should advise students to become very familiar with the reading assignments so they know what is expected of them.

<u>Extra Activities Center</u>   The Unit Resource Materials portion of this LitPlan contains suggestions for an extra library of related books and articles in your classroom as well as crossword and word search puzzles. Make an extra activities center in your room where you will keep these materials for students to use. (Bring the books and articles in from the library and keep several copies of the puzzles on hand.) Explain to students that these materials are available for students to use when they finish reading assignments or other class work early.

<u>Nonfiction Assignment Sheet</u>   Explain to students that they each are to read at least one non-fiction piece from the in-class library at some time during the unit. Students will fill out a nonfiction assignment sheet after completing the reading to help you (the teacher) evaluate their reading experiences and to help the students think about and evaluate their own reading experiences.

<u>Books</u>   Each school has its own rules and regulations regarding student use of school books. Advise students of the procedures that are normal for your school. Preview the book. Look at the covers, front-matter, and index.

WRITING ASSIGNMENT #1: *Antigone*
Interpretive: writing a tragedy based on a Greek myth

PROMPT:
Sophocles' *Antigone* follows the structure of a Greek tragedy, and contains each of the following:
  I. **Prologue:** Spoken by one or two characters before the chorus appears. The prologue usually gives the background information needed to understand the events of the play.
  II. **Parodos:** the song sung by the chorus as it makes its entrance
  III. **Episodes/Scenes:** the main action of the play
  IV. **Odes:** a song (and often dance) that reflects on the events of the episodes, and puts the plot into some kind of larger mythological framework
     A. *Choragos:* the leader of the chorus who often interacts with the characters in the scenes.
     B. *Chorus:* the singers/dancers who remark on the action
        1. strophe: the movement of the chorus from right to left across the stage
        2. antistrophe: the reaction to the strophe, which moves across the stage from left to right.
  V. **Paean:** a prayer of thanksgiving to Dionysos in whose honor the Greek plays were performed
  VI. **Exodos:** sung by the chorus as it makes its final exit, which usually offers words of wisdom related to the actions and outcome of the play

PREWRITING:
Your group has selected one of the following myths and you will re-tell the story in the format of a Greek tragedy.

Cupid and Psyche	Echo
Pandora's box	Callisto and Arcas
Hercules (before his twelve labors)	Atreus
Narcissus	Orpheus

DRAFTING:
Each member of your group will work *individually* on a specific *section* of the tragedy (other than the odes), and you will ALL work on creating the odes. (There are as many odes as there are scenes in the play.) You must have at least two scenes in your tragedy. You will have time to work as a group to brainstorm ideas for what should be included in each of the individual sections, but the actual writing will be done independently. The creation of the odes will be part of a separate lesson. At least four of the vocabulary words from the unit must be incorporated into each portion.

Individual Work Division:
   prologue and parodos
   scene 1
   scene 2
   paean and exodos

PEER CONFERENCE/REVISING
When you finish the draft, ask another student to look at it. You may want to give the student your pre-writing notes and scenario so he/she can double check to see you have included all the information you intended to include. After reading, he/she should tell you what is best about your essay, which parts were difficult to understand or follow, and ways in which your essay could be improved. Reread your essay considering your critic's comments and make the corrections you think are necessary. You will be completing a peer editing form in Lesson 4.
Do a final proofreading of your essay, double-checking your grammar, spelling, organization, and the clarity of your ideas.

LESSON TWO

Objectives:
- Students will become familiar with the Oedipus story which is featured in the background of *Antigone*.
- Students will have the opportunity to use the library/media center in order to complete their non-fiction assignment.
- Studens will preview the vocabulary and study questions for the Prologue and the Parodos.
- Studends will begin reading *Antigone*.

Activity #1:
    Tell the story of Oedipus (it is easily found in the library or on the Internet) and have students identify the elements of this tragic tale. Write these elements on the board. What is it about Oedipus that leads to his tragic downfall? What parts of the story are out of his control? What parts ARE under his control and how does that lead to the denouement? Explain that Antigone is one of Oedipus' daughters, and have students predict what impact Oedipus' tale might have on Antigone.

Activity #2:
Give each student a non-fiction assignment sheet. Students will use the library/media center to find articles about the history of Greek Theatre in order to complete the assignment sheet. In addition to the questions on the sheet itself, students must provide a definition for each of the following as well as a brief discussion of its importance to Greek Theatre:
- Dionysus and the Dionysia
- Thespis
- Aeschylus
- Satyr
- The Use of Masks

Activity #3:
Tell students that prior to your next class meeting, they should preview the study questions and do the vocabulary worksheet for the Prologue and the Parodos and then read it.

NOTE: Depending on the level of your class, this lesson may take more than one class period.

NONFICTION ASSIGNMENT SHEET
(To be completed after reading the required nonfiction article/s)

Name _____ Date _____

Title of Nonfiction Read _____

Written By _____ Publication Date _____

I. Factual Summary: Write a short summary of the piece you read.

II. Vocabulary
    1. With which vocabulary words in the piece did you encounter some degree of difficulty?

    2. How did you resolve your lack of understanding with these words?

III. Interpretation: What was the main point the author wanted you to get from reading his work?

IV. Criticism
    1. With which points of the piece did you agree or find easy to accept? Why?

    2. With which points of the piece did you disagree or find difficult to believe? Why?

V. Personal Response: What do you think about this piece? OR How does this piece influence your ideas?

LESSON THREE

Objectives:
- Students will be able to demonstrate reading comprehension through sharing responses to the study guide questions.
- Students will practice public speaking skills by reading and performing aloud.

Activity #1:

Give students a few minutes to formulate answers for the study guide questions for the Prologue and the Parodos, and then discuss the answers to the questions in detail. Write the answers on the board or overhead transparency so students can have the correct answers for study purposes. Note: It is a good practice in public speaking and leadership skills for individual students to take charge of leading the discussions of the study questions. Perhaps a different student could go to the front of the class and lead the discussion each day that the study questions are discussed during this unit. Of course, the teacher should guide the discussion when appropriate and be sure to fill in any gaps the students leave.

Activity #2:

Allow students to work independently on the vocabulary sheets and the study questions for Scene 1 and Ode 1.

Activity #3:

Cast the characters of *Antigone* for the Prologue through the first Ode. You probably know the best way to get readers with your class; pick students at random, ask for volunteers, or use whatever method works best for your group. All of the students who are NOT cast as specific characters will be in the chorus. Be sure that those who formulate the chorus are divided into the strophe and the antistrophe, and that they move across the "stage" accordingly. If you have not yet completed an oral reading evaluation for your students this period, this would be a good opportunity to do so. A form is included with this unit for your convenience.

NOTE: Remind students to bring in their drafts of the mythology project to the next class for a peer edit.

ORAL READING EVALUATION - *Antigone*

Name _____ Class____ Date _____

SKILL	EXCELLENT	GOOD	AVERAGE	FAIR	POOR
Fluency	5	4	3	2	1
Clarity	5	4	3	2	1
Audibility	5	4	3	2	1
Pronunciation	5	4	3	2	1
_____	5	4	3	2	1
_____	5	4	3	2	1

Total _____   Grade _____

Comments:

LESSON FOUR

Objectives:
- Students will be able to demonstrate reading comprehension through sharing responses to study guide questions.
- Students will demonstrate their understanding of the play by taking a quiz.
- Students will further develop co-operative learning skills through group work.
- Students will participate in a peer editing session.

Activity #1:
   Give students a few minutes to formulate answers for the study guide questions for Scene1 and Ode 1, and then discuss the answers to the questions in detail. Write the answers on the board or overhead transparency so students can have the correct answers for study purposes.

Activity #2:
   Quiz - Distribute quizzes for the Prologue through Ode 1, and give students about 10 minutes to complete them.

NOTE: The quizzes may either be the short answer study guides or the multiple choice version. Have students exchange papers. Grade the quizzes as a class. Collect the papers for recording the grades. If you used the multiple choice version as a quiz, take a few minutes to discuss the answers for the short answer version if your students are using the short answer version for their study guides.

Activity #3:
   Allow mythology groups to get together to work on their tragedies. Each member should have a draft and the group members should exchange written pieces for a peer edit. A peer editing sheet is contained in this unit for your convenience.

Activity #4:
   Tell students to preview the study questions and do the vocabulary worksheet for Scene 2 and Ode 2, and then read it prior to the next class meeting.

NOTE: If your students can't handle the previewing and reading independently as homework, make class time for it by adding days in between the lessons given.

PEER WRITING EDITING FORM
GREEK MYTHOLOGY TRAGEDIES

Editor's Name _____ Writer's Name _____ Date _____
Assignment _____

A. Does the writer's piece fit the portion of the tragedy he/she was assigned to write?
   If your answer is "yes", be sure to tell the writer what he/she did that you especially liked. If your answer is "no," tell the writer what he/she could have included in order to write a better essay.

Editor:
_____
_____

Writer:
_____
_____

B. Did he/she provide enough details to set the scenes that will follow (stage directions, descriptions of characters, etc)?

   If your answer is "yes", be sure to tell the writer what you especially liked about his/her response. If your answer is "no", you must tell the writer how he/she could improve his/her response (adding specific details that were missed, connecting to position better, or adding embedded quotations).

Editor:
_____
_____

Writer:
_____
_____

C. Identify sentence type
   Be sure to know the difference between simple, simple with compound subject, simple with compound predicate, compound, complex, and compound-complex. Using the first body paragraph, correctly identify each sentence type. If there is sufficient sentence structure variety, tell the writer what he/she did well. If not, explain what he/she could have done differently. Characters should not speak in choppy, simple sentences.

   Sentence 1: _____   *Sentence 5:* _____
   Sentence 2: _____   *Sentence 6:* _____
   Sentence 3: _____   *Sentence 7:* _____
   Sentence 4: _____   *Sentence 8:* _____

Editor:
_____
_____

Writer:
_____
_____

Antigone Peer Editing Continued

D. Address the Focus Correction Areas
    Did the writer follow the specifics of the assignment such as (address each individually):

    1. Organization:

    Editor: _____

    Writer: _____

    2. Use of vocabulary words as directed:

    Editor: _____

    Writer: _____

    3. Stays true to original myth:

    Editor: _____

    Writer: _____

E. Check for errors in grammar, spelling, punctuation, etc.

Editor: _____

Writer: _____

LESSON FIVE

Objectives:
- Students will be able to demonstrate reading comprehension through sharing responses to study guide questions.
- Students will have the opportunity to practice public speaking skills by reading and performing aloud.

Activity #1:
Give students a few minutes to formulate answers for the study guide questions for Scene 2 and Ode 2, and then discuss the answers to the questions in detail. Write the answers on the board or overhead transparency so students can have the correct answers for study purposes.

Activity #2:
Cast the characters of *Antigone* for Scene 2 through Ode 3. You probably know the best way to get readers with your class; pick students at random, ask for volunteers, or use whatever method works best for your group. Be sure that those who formulate the chorus (all of the students who are NOT cast as specific characters will be in the chorus) are divided into the strophe and the antistrophe, and that they move across the "stage" accordingly. If you have not yet completed an oral reading evaluation for your students this period, this would be a good opportunity to do so. A form is included with this unit for your convenience.

Activity #3:
Allow students to work in groups in the creation of the masks that will be needed for their group performances. Mardi-Gras half-masks work well for this project, and they can be purchased cheaply on the Internet or you can get them at a craft store. You could also ask students in advance to purchase their own plain masks and then decorate them in class. Be sure to have on hand (students could also be asked to bring in contributions, or ask the Art department for any spare materials):

- glue
- scissors
- sequins
- beads
- feathers
- poster paint
- glitter
- construction paper

The masks should contain symbolic representations of the characters they will be portraying in their tragedies. Students should make sure that they have decided who will play/memorize which part in their productions.

Activity #4:
Tell students to preview the study questions and do the vocabulary worksheet for Scene 3 and Ode 3, and then read it prior to the next class meeting.

LESSON SIX

Objectives:
- Students will be able to demonstrate reading comprehension through sharing responses to study guide questions.
- Students will demonstrate understanding of the play through taking a quiz.
- Students will work in cooperative groups as they analyze Sophocles' use of characterization in his tragedy.

Activity #1:

Give students a few minutes to formulate answers for the study guide questions for Scene 3 and Ode 3, and then discuss the answers to the questions in detail. Write the answers on the board or overhead transparency so students can have the correct answers for study purposes.

Activity #2:

Quiz - Distribute quizzes for Scene 2 through Ode 3, and give students about 10 minutes to complete them.
(Note: The quizzes may either be the short answer study guides or the multiple choice version.) Have students exchange papers. Grade the quizzes as a class. Collect the papers for recording the grades. (If you used the multiple choice version as a quiz, take a few minutes to discuss the answers for the short answer version if your students are using the short answer version for their study guides.)

Activity #3:

Divide students into 6 groups–one for each of the following: Antigone, Ismene, King Creon, Haimon, the Choragos, the Chorus

Each group will be given a large sheet of construction paper to be used to create a character poster. On each poster, the groups must provide the following:
- the name of the character
- a labeled picture of the character based on the physical description given in the text
- a list of at least three positive character traits with supporting evidence and corresponding scene and line numbers for each
- a list of at least three negative character traits with supporting evidence and corresponding scene and line numbers for each

* NOTE: treat the chorus and the choragus as though they were individual characters, and use the odes to characterize them. As for physical description, use what you know about the Greek theatre to draw them.

Activity #4

After students finish their posters, each pair/group must get up in front of the class and share the information about its particular character. Those who are not presenting must take notes about the other characters. Remind students that they will all be responsible for being able to identify all of the characters on the unit test.

Activity #5:

Tell students to preview the study questions and do the vocabulary worksheet for Scene 4 and Ode 4, and then read it prior to the next class meeting.

LESSON SEVEN

Objectives:
- Students will be able to demonstrate reading comprehension through sharing responses to study guide questions.
- Students will have the opportunity to use the library/media center to begin their research papers about the life of Sophocles

Activity #1:

Give students a few minutes to formulate answers for the study guide questions for Scene 4 and Ode 4, and then discuss the answers to the questions in detail. Write the answers on the board or overhead transparency so students can have the correct answers for study purposes.

Activity #2:

Distribute Writing Assignment #2 (informative piece) about the life of Sophocles (other than as a playwright). Take students to the library/media center where they can begin their research in preparation for this assignment.

Activity #3:

Students may work in groups on their mythology projects if they have time.

Activity #4:

Tell students to preview the study questions and do the vocabulary worksheet for Scene 5 and then read it prior to the next class meeting.

WRITING ASSIGNMENT #2 – *Antigone*
Informational: The Life of Sophocles

PROMPT
You are reading the Greek tragedy *Antigone* by Sophocles, and the class has been exploring Sophocles' influence in the Greek Theatre. Although Sophocles was an award-winning playwright, he contributed much more to his society. Research how Sophocles contributed to the theatre *beyond* the role of playwright, as well as to his society in each of the following roles: priest, politician, and soldier.

PREWRITING
After researching the required information at the library/media center, use your findings to write a report about Sophocles' accomplishments and contributions to the Greek society. You must support your ideas with quotations from your sources and cite them correctly.

DRAFTING
Introduce your topic in the first paragraph, being sure to end with a thesis statement. Then write several body paragraphs, each describing Sophocles various roles in and contributions to his society. Be sure to include embedded quotations from your research as support for your thesis. Also, incorporate at least four vocabulary words from the unit into your essay. Finally, conclude by making modern connections to those involved in the entertainment industry who have made significant contributions to society. End the conclusion by challenging your reader in some way.

PEER CONFERENCE/REVISING
When you finish the draft, ask another student to look at it. You may want to give the student your worksheets and articles so he/she can double check to see you have included all the information you intended to include. After reading, he/she should tell you what is best about your essay, which parts were difficult to understand or follow, and ways in which your essay could be improved. Reread your essay considering your critic's comments and make the corrections you think are necessary.

PROOFREADING/EDITING
Do a final proofreading of your essay, double-checking your grammar, spelling, organization, and the clarity of your ideas.

WRITING EVALUATION FORM - *Antigone*

Name _____ Date _____

Grade _____

Circle One For Each Item:

Grammar: correct errors noted on paper

Spelling: correct errors noted on paper

Punctuation: correct errors noted on paper

Legibility: excellent   good   fair   poor

_____   excellent   good   fair   poor

_____   excellent   good   fair   poor

Strengths:

Weaknesses:

Comments/Suggestions:

LESSON EIGHT

Objectives:
- Students will be able to demonstrate reading comprehension through sharing responses to study guide questions.
- Students will have the opportunity to practice public speaking skills by reading and performing aloud.
- Students will have the opportunity to work independently.

Activity #1:

Give students a few minutes to formulate answers for the study guide questions for Scene 5, and then discuss the answers to the questions in detail. Write the answers on the board or overhead transparency so students can have the correct answers for study purposes.

Activity #2:

Cast the characters of *Antigone* for Scene 4 through the Exodos. You probably know the best way to get readers with your class; pick students at random, ask for volunteers, or use whatever method works best for your group. Be sure that those who formulate the chorus (all of the students who are NOT cast as specific characters will be in the chorus) are divided into the strophe and the antistrophe, and that they move across the "stage" accordingly. If you have not yet completed an oral reading evaluation for your students this period, this would be a good opportunity to do so. A form is included with this unit for your convenience.

Activity #3:

Allow students to independently work on the vocabulary exercises and the study questions for the Paean and the Exodos.

LESSON NINE

Objectives:
- Students will be able to demonstrate reading comprehension through sharing responses to study guide questions.
- Students will have the opportunity to demonstrate understanding of the play through taking a quiz.
- Students will have the opportunity to demonstrate their understanding of persuasive speech (logos, pathos, and ethos) and apply what they know to *Antigone*.

Activity #1:

Give students a few minutes to formulate answers for the study guide questions for the Paean and the Exodos, and then discuss the answers to the questions in detail. Write the answers on the board or overhead transparency so students can have the correct answers for study purposes.

Activity #2:

Quiz - Distribute quizzes for Scene 4 through the Exodos, and give students about 10 minutes to complete them.
(Note: The quizzes may either be the short answer study guides or the multiple choice version.) Have students exchange papers. Grade the quizzes as a class. Collect the papers for recording the grades. (If you used the multiple choice version as a quiz, take a few minutes to discuss the answers for the short answer version if your students are using the short answer version for their study guides.)

Activity #3:

Discuss the following rhetorical devices used in persuasive speech: logos (appealing to one's sense of reason), pathos (tugging at the heart strings), and ethos (appealing to one's sense of moral obligation). Define each, and ask students to give examples of each from real life, television, movies, or literature. Write their responses on the board under the proper heading (logos, pathos, ethos) and ask them to explain why the responses fit that particular rhetorical device.

Activity #4:

Divide the class into 5 groups and assign each group one of the following scenes from *Antigone*. Each group is to read the scene and then look for evidence of the three rhetorical devices mentioned used by the various characters in an attempt to persuade another.
1. the Prologue between Antigone and Ismene
2. Scene 1 between King Creon and the Choragos
3. Scene 2 between King Creon and Antigone
4. Scene 3 between King Creon and Haimon
5. Scene 5 between Teiresias and King Creon

Have each group present its findings to the rest of the class.

LESSON TEN

Objectives:
- Students will recognize the use of figurative language in modern (not ancient Greek) odes as well as be able to define an ode as a poetic form.
- Students will analyze the four odes in Sophocles' *Antigone* for the use of figurative language by the poet.
- Students will work in their mythology groups to create odes for their own Greek tragedies.

Activity #1:

Pass out copies and read aloud "Ode on a Grecian Urn" by John Keats. Ask students to try to define what an *ode* is. (The definition of an ode is a poem praising and glorifying a person, place or thing. Also, a copy of Keats' poem is included in this LitPlan since it has gone into public domain). What is Keats praising in his poem? Ask students to re-read the first stanza and identify as many uses of figurative language/poetic devices that they can find (imagery, symbolism, simile, metaphor, personification, allusion, etc). Go through the first stanza together as a class, and then break the class up into four groups. Assign each group one of the four remaining stanzas and have them repeat the process. Have the groups share their findings with the rest of the class and explain how each poetic device enhances the poem as a whole.

Activity #2:

Using the same four groups, assign one of the odes from *Antigone* to each group and repeat the process. What is being praised/glorified in each? What poetic devices does Sophocles use in his odes and how do they affect the poem as a whole? Again, students share their findings and encourage all to take notes that they can study for the unit test.

Activity #3:

Have students get into their mythology groups and begin creating the odes that will be used in their productions. Remember that there is a minimum of two scenes (besides the prologue, parodos, paean, and exodus) for each of their plays, so there will be one ode for each scene. Students must use at least four types of figurative language/poetic devices in each ode.

John Keats
"Ode On a Grecian Urn" (1819)
I
Thou still unravish'd bride of quietness,
   Thou foster-child of silence and slow time,
Sylvan historian, who canst thus express
   A flowery tale more sweetly than our rhyme:
What leaf-fring'd legend haunts about thy shape   5
   Of deities or mortals, or of both,
      In Tempe or the dales of Arcady?
   What men or gods are these? What maidens loth?
What mad pursuit? What struggle to escape?
      What pipes and timbrels? What wild ecstasy   10

II
Heard melodies are sweet, but those unheard
   Are sweeter; therefore, ye soft pipes, play on;
Not to the sensual ear, but, more endeared,
   Pipe to the spirit ditties of no tone:
Fair youth, beneath the trees, thou canst not leave   15
   Thy song, nor ever can those trees be bare;
Bold Lover, never, never canst thou kiss,
Though winning near the goal-- yet, do not grieve;
She cannot fade, though thou hast not thy bliss,
For ever wilt thou love, and she be fair!   20

III
Ah, happy, happy boughs! that cannot shed
   Your leaves, nor ever bid the Spring adieu;
And, happy melodist, unwearied,
   For ever piping songs for ever new;
More happy love! more happy, happy love!   25
   For ever warm and still to be enjoy'd,
      For ever panting, and for ever young;
All breathing human passion far above,
   That leaves a heart high-sorrowful and cloy'd,
      A burning forehead, and a parching tongue.   30

"Ode To A Grecian Urn" Continued

IV
Who are these coming to the sacrifice?
   To what green altar, O mysterious priest,
Lead'st thou that heifer lowing at the skies,
   And all her silken flanks with garlands dressed?
What little town by river or sea shore,   35
   Or mountain-built with peaceful citadel,
      Is emptied of this folk, this pious morn?
And, little town, thy streets for evermore
   Will silent be; and not a soul to tell
      Why thou art desolate, can e'er return.   40

V
O Attic shape! Fair attitude! with brede
   Of marble men and maidens overwrought,
With forest branches and the trodden weed;
   Thou, silent form, dost tease us out of thought
As doth eternity: Cold Pastoral!   45
   When old age shall this generation waste,
      Thou shalt remain, in midst of other woe
   Than ours, a friend to man, to whom thou say'st,
"Beauty is truth, truth beauty,-- that is all
   Ye know on earth, and all ye need to know."   50

LESSON ELEVEN

Objectives:
- Students will work in co-operative groups to complete their mythology projects

Activity:

Have students get into their mythology groups. They are to work on polishing up the dialogue for each of the parts of the play, as well as complete their masks (if they have not already done so), and to finalize their odes.

Students may take the opportunity to rehearse their plays in various parts of the room.

LESSON TWELVE

Objective
To review all of the vocabulary work done in this unit

Activity
Choose one (or more) of the vocabulary review activities listed below and spend your class period as directed in the activity. Some of the materials for these review activities are located in the Vocabulary Resource Materials section in this LitPlan.

VOCABULARY REVIEW ACTIVITIES

1. Divide your class into two teams and have an old-fashioned spelling or definition bee.

2. Give each of your students (or students in groups of two, three or four) an *Antigone* Vocabulary Word Search Puzzle. The person (group) to find all of the vocabulary words in the puzzle first wins.

3. Give students an *Antigone* Vocabulary Word Search Puzzle without the word list. The person or group to find the most vocabulary words in the puzzle wins.

4. Use an *Antigone* Vocabulary Crossword Puzzle. Put the puzzle onto a transparency on the overhead projector (so everyone can see it), and do the puzzle together as a class.

5. Give students an *Antigone* Vocabulary Matching Worksheet to do.

6. Divide your class into two teams. Use *Antigone* vocabulary words with their letters jumbled as a word list. Student 1 from Team A faces off against Student 1 from Team B. You write the first jumbled word on the board. The first student (1A or 1B) to unscramble the word wins the chance for his/her team to score points. If 1A wins the jumble, go to student 2A and give him/her a definition. He/she must give you the correct spelling of the vocabulary word which fits that definition. If he/she does, Team A scores a point, and you give student 3A a definition for which you expect a correctly spelled matching vocabulary word. Continue giving Team A definitions until some team member makes an incorrect response. An incorrect response sends the game back to the jumbled-word face off, this time with students 2A and 2B. Instead of repeating giving definitions to the first few students of each team, continue with the student after the one who gave the last incorrect response on the team. For example, if Team B wins the jumbled-word face-off, and student 5B gave the last incorrect answer for Team B, you would start this round of definition questions with student 6B, and so on. The team with the most points wins!

7. Have students write a story in which they correctly use as many vocabulary words as possible. Have students read their compositions orally! Post the most original compositions on your bulletin board!

8.. Play *I Have, Who Has?* *NOTE This requires preparation in advance. On 3x5 cards, write a vocabulary word on one side and a definition to another word on the other side of the card. Once you have completed a set, pass that cards out randomly, keeping one for yourself. You will start the game by saying, "Who Has..." and reading the definition on the card. The student who has the word on his/her card that matches the definition shouts, "I Have..." and reads the word. He/She then turns over the card and says "Who Has..." and play continues until the all the words/cards have been gone through.

LESSON THIRTEEN

Objective:
- Students will demonstrate an understanding of the play beyond the factual questions asked in the study guide.

Activity:

Choose the questions from the Extra Discussion Questions/Writing Assignments which seem most appropriate for your students. A class discussion of these questions is most effective if students have been given the opportunity to formulate answers to the questions prior to the discussion. To this end, you may either have all the students formulate answers to all the questions, divide your class into groups and assign one or more questions to each group, or you could assign one question to each student in your class. The option you choose will make a difference in the amount of class time needed for this activity.

NOTE: The use of graphic organizers may be helpful to students in preparing their answers. Encourage them to use any diagrams or graphics that they feel are necessary.

EXTRA DISCUSSION QUESTIONS/WRITING ASSIGNMENTS - *Antigone*

Interpretation
1. At the end of the Parodos, the Chorus has certain expectations for the future Thebes after the war. What are these expectations? Explain whether or not these expectations were met by the end of the play.
2. Summarize Creon's "state of the union address." What are his specific hopes for Thebes?
3. What motivates Creon to stick to his decision regarding his decree? What is Antigone's motivation for her decision? What motivates Haimon to defend Antigone?
4. How do Antigone's final lines in scene 4 foreshadow Creon's fate?
5. Where is the climax of this play? Support your choice.

Critical
1. Fully explain why King Creon does not want Polyneices buried.
2. What does Creon mean when he says, "An enemy is an enemy, even dead"?
3. What seems to be the attitude toward women throughout this play? Support with evidence from the text.
4. Discuss the playwright's use of dramatic irony throughout the tragedy.
5. Explain the two metaphors that Haimon uses in his attempt to persuade his father to be merciful to Antigone.
6. Revisit the use of rhetorical devices of persuasion already discussed regarding the play.
    a. the Prologue between Antigone and Ismene
    b. Scene 1 between King Creon and the Choragos
    c. Scene 2 between King Creon and Antigone
    d. Scene 3 between King Creon and Haimon
    e. Scene 5 between Teiresias and King Creon
   Find other examples of the use of logos, pathos, or ethos in the tragedy.
7. Why is it particularly ironic that Teiresias, the prophet, is blind?
8. How does the fact that certain character refuse to appear weak affect the outcome of this play? What seems to be Sophocles' message about pride?
9. For each of the following characters, select an object and explain how that object could be used to symbolize that person's particular character traits:
    - Antigone
    - Haimon
    - Teiresias
    - Creon
    - Ismene
    - Polyneices

Critical/Personal Response
1. What is your initial reaction to Antigone's character based on her interaction with Ismene in the Prologue? List her positive and negative traits, using textual support as evidence.
2. The Ancient Greeks had certain customs regarding the burial of the dead. Based on the play, what do these customs seem to be and what is the purpose of them? How do they compare to burial customs in your society? Research burial customs in at least two cultures other than your own. What differences do you find? Similarities?

Antigone Extra Discussion Questions Continued

3. Many famous people in history have stood up for what they believe is right, yet have been arrested for doing so. Research the following and tell what each believed in, and what he/she did that caused him/her to be arrested?
   - Dr. Martin Luther King, Jr.
   - Mahatma Ghandi
   - Rosa Parks
   - Henry David Thoreau
3. Haimon claims that the people of Thebes only follow Creon out of fear. Think of examples of others who have only gone along with something/someone because they were afraid of the consequences of NOT going along.
4. Lord Acton once said, "Absolute power corrupts absolutely." How can that statement be reflected in *Antigone*?
5. Suppose King Creon had reached Antigone's vault in time to save her. How might the play have had a different ending?
6. Suppose Haimon had actually killed Creon instead of missing him. What different direction might the play have taken?
7. Make of list of movies that could fit into the category of a tragedy. What elements are present in these movies that make them fit into this genre?

Personal Response
1. Is it always important to obey every law? Explain why or why not, and give examples to support your answer.
2. If you were in Antigone's place, what would you do? What about Creon's place?
3. Are you intrigued about the story of Oedipus that seems to run in the background of this play? Do you intend to read about it? Why or why not?

LESSON FOURTEEN

Objectives:
- Students will have an opportunity to demonstrate their writing skills through the completion of an in-class writing assignment.
- Students will have the opportunity to demonstrate the skills of persuasive speech from lesson nine (logos, pathos, and ethos)

Activity #1:

Distribute the writing assignment to each student and read over it aloud. Give students the remaining time to write the essay in class.

Reminder:

Logos: appealing to one's sense of logical reasoning
Pathos: appealing to one's emotions; tugging at the heart strings
Ethos: appealing to one's sense of moral duty/obligation

Activity #2:

In the event students finish early, they may work on more of the Extra Discussion Questions or work independently editing their portion of the tragedy written in groups.

WRITING ASSIGNMENT #3 - *Antigone*
Persuasive: Moral Dilemmas

PROMPT
You have finished reading the Greek tragedy *Antigone* by Sophocles, and the class has been exploring the conflicts introduced in the play. Although Sophocles lived in Ancient Greece, people today are still faced with moral dilemmas.

PREWRITING
Define the concept and discuss Antigone's moral dilemma. Select one of the two scenarios below and describe the moral dilemma being faced. After carefully thinking about the problem, decide what you would do in that same situation. Then write an essay defending your position and attempt to persuade your reader to believe that you made the best, moral choice. In your argument, use the rhetorical devices of logos, pathos, and ethos to try to persuade your reader.

Moral Dilemmas:
1. Your sister's child has a terrible ear infection and she cannot get an appointment with the doctor until the next day. When you call your sister to see how your niece is doing, you hear her crying in the background. You know that your sister does not have a prescription, but you happen to work as a pharmacist and you know what kind of an antibiotic she probably needs. What do you do?
2. Your husband lost his job six months ago not long after the two of you had finally purchased the home of your dreams. He's been looking for work, but has not been able to find anything that will pay enough to allow you to keep the house. On the day your house is being foreclosed on, you happen to find a large envelope lying on the ground outside the law firm. The name on the envelope is the name of the lawyer who is handling the foreclosure case against you and it happens to contain $10,000 in cash. What do you do?

DRAFTING
Introduce your topic in the first paragraph, being sure to end with a thesis statement. In your body paragraphs, make sure that you discuss Antigone's moral dilemma, describe the situation of the dilemma you have been presented with, your position on the situation, and your use of rhetoric as you persuade your reader. Be sure to incorporate at least four vocabulary words from the unit into your essay. End the conclusion by challenging your reader in some way.

PEER CONFERENCE/REVISING
When you finish the draft, ask another student to look at it. You may want to give the student your pre-writing notes and scenario so he/she can double check to see you have included all the information you intended to include. After reading, he/she should tell you what is best about your essay, which parts were difficult to understand or follow, and ways in which your essay could be improved. Reread your essay considering your critic's comments and make the corrections you think are necessary. You will be completing a peer editing form the next class.
Do a final proofreading of your essay, double-checking your grammar, spelling, organization, and the clarity of your ideas.

LESSON FIFTEEN

Objectives:
1. Students will demonstrate their ability to assess another's writing thorough a peer editing exercise.
2. Students will demonstrate their ability to accept constructive criticism and make changes in their writing when necessary.

Activity #1

Put students in pairs for peer editing and give each student a peer writing evaluation form. Students will exchange their persuasive essays written in class the day before and make comments regarding content, language use, and conventions (under "Editor"). Students will return the essays to the writer and then they respond to their peer's comments about their own writing on the editing sheet (under "Writer"). After thanking his/her peer for their comments, the writer will revise and rewrite the essay to turn in for a grade.

Activity #2

Once students have edited and revised their writing and turned the essays in to be graded, they may work on finishing their projects for the upcoming presentations.

LESSONS SIXTEEN and SEVENTEEN

Objectives:
- Students will have the opportunity to practice public speaking skills through the presentations of their group tragedies.
- Students will have the opportunity to demonstrate their knowledge of the structure of a Greek tragedy through their presentations.

Activity #1:

There will probably be time for four of the groups to present each day. Distribute enough copies for each student to evaluate the plays that they will be watching being performed. Each student will evaluate the group's presentation and provide feedback for their peers. The teacher, of course, will be evaluating as well. A group presentation evaluation sheet has been provided for your convenience.

Activity #2:

If there is any remaining time, the teacher can provide further vocabulary review materials or any of the other review materials in preparation for the unit test.

GROUP PRESENTATION EVALUATION SHEET

Each of the following will be graded on a scale of 1-5, with 1 being the lowest; each is worth 20% of the overall grade.

- Part I: individual contribution during the preparation time in class (which has been monitored during media center visit and in-class group work)
- Part II: individual contribution to the group project/performance (how well he/she has memorized or is at least prepared to read from a script his/her part)
- Part III: individual contributed correct format to the class based on the structure of a Greek tragedy
- Part IV: individual portion of the play remains true to the original Greek myth
- Part V: individual has provided all of his/her necessary portion of the group project (this includes the creation of mask)

Group Topic: _____

Student Name	Part I	Part II	Part III	Part IV	Part V	Total Score

LESSON EIGHTEEN

REVIEW GAMES/ACTIVITIES - *Antigone*

1. Ask the class to make up a unit test for *Antigone*. The test should have 4 sections: matching, true/false, short answer, and essay. Students may use 1/2 period to make the test and then swap papers and use the other 1/2 class period to take a test a classmate has devised. (open book) You may want to use the unit test included in this packet or take questions from the students' unit tests to formulate your own test.

2. Take 1/2 period for students to make up true and false questions (including the answers). Collect the papers and divide the class into two teams. Draw a big tic-tac-toe board on the chalk board. Make one team X and one team O. Ask questions to each side, giving each student one turn. If the question is answered correctly, that students' team's letter (X or O) is placed in the box. If the answer is incorrect, no letter is placed in the box. The object is to get three in a row like tic-tac-toe. You may want to keep track of the number of games won for each team.

3. Take 1/2 period for students to make up questions (true/false and short answer). Collect the questions. Divide the class into two teams. You'll alternate asking questions to individual members of teams A & B (like in a spelling bee). The question keeps going from A to B until it is correctly answered, then a new question is asked. A correct answer does not allow the team to get another question. Correct answers are +2 points; incorrect answers are -1 point.

4. Have students pair up and quiz each other from their study guides and class notes.

5. Give students an *Antigone* crossword puzzle to complete.

6. Divide your class into two teams. Use *Antigone* crossword words with their letters jumbled as a word list. Student 1 from Team A faces off against Student 1 from Team B. You write the first jumbled word on the board. The first student (1A or 1B) to unscramble the word wins the chance for his/her team to score points. If 1A wins the jumble, go to student 2A and give him/her a clue. He/she must give you the correct word which matches that clue. If he/she does, Team A scores a point, and you give student 3A a clue for which you expect another correct response. Continue giving Team A clues until some team member makes an incorrect response. An incorrect response sends the game back to the jumbled-word face off, this time with students 2A and 2B. Instead of repeating giving clues to the first few students of each team, continue with the student after the one who gave the last incorrect response on the team. For example, if Team B wins the jumbled-word face-off, and student 5B gave the last incorrect answer for Team B, you would start this round of clue questions with student 6B, and so on. The team with the most points wins!

7. Play *What's My Line?*. This is similar to the old television show. Students assume the roles of different characters from the tragedy. One student gives clues to the class, or to a panel of contestants. The contestants try to guess the identity of the guest. Students may enjoy assisting you in creating rules and procedures for the game.

8. Play *Jeopardy*. Divide the class into two groups. Assign each group a category or scene from the play and have them devise answers for that category. Play the game according to the television show procedures.

9. Play *Drawing in the Details*. This is similar to Pictionary. Divide students into teams. A student from one team draws a scene from the tragedy. (You may want to specify the scene or ode.) Drawings should be kept simple, to keep the pace lively. Students in the opposing team locate the scene in their books and read it aloud. If they are incorrect, the illustrator's team has a chance to guess. Involve students in setting up a scoring system and any other necessary rules.

10. Play *I Have, Who Has?* *NOTE This requires preparation in advance. On 3x5 cards, write a clue word on one side and a clue/definition/question to another clue word on the other side of the card. Once you have completed a set, pass that cards out randomly, keeping one for yourself. You will start the game by saying, "Who Has…" and reading the definition/question on the card. The student who has the answer on his/her card that matches the definition/question shouts, "I Have…" and reads the answer. He/She then turns over the card and says "Who Has…" and play continues until the all the cards have been gone through.

LESSON NINETEEN - *Antigone*

<u>Objective</u>
To test the students understanding of the main ideas and themes in *Antigone*

<u>Activity #1</u>
Distribute the unit tests. Go over the instructions in detail and allow the students the entire class period to complete the exam.

NOTES ABOUT THE TESTS IN THIS UNIT:

There are 5 different unit tests which follow.

There are two short answer tests which are based primarily on facts from the tragedy. The answer key for short answer unit test 1 follows the student test. The answer key for short answer test 2 follows the student short answer unit test 2.

There is one advanced short answer unit test, and it is based on the extra discussion questions. The answer key to the matching section follows the advanced short answer unit test. There is no key for the short answer questions. The answers will be based on the discussions you have had during class.

There are two multiple choice unit tests. Following the two unit tests, you will find an answer sheet on which students should mark their answers. The same answer sheet should be used for both tests; however, students' answers will be different for each test. Following the students' answer sheet for the multiple choice tests you will find your two keys: one for multiple choice test 1 and one for multiple choice test 2.

The short answer tests have a vocabulary section. You should choose 10 of the vocabulary words from this unit, read them orally and have the students write them down. Then, either have students write a definition or use the words in sentences.

Use these words for the vocabulary section of the advanced short answer unit test:

auspicious	anarchists	lithe	insolence
transcends	deference	subordinate	blasphemy
dirges	implacable	augury	aphorism

<u>Activity #2</u>
Collect all test papers and assigned books prior to the end of the class period.

UNIT TESTS

SHORT ANSWER UNIT TEST 1 - *Antigone*

I. Matching/Identify

____ 1. Polyneices A. a blind prophet

____ 2. Creon B. Oedipus' son who was buried with full honors by the state

____ 3. Oedipus C. killed his father and married his mother; father of Antigone

____ 4. Ismene D. a scene in a play

____ 5. Haimon E. the queen of Thebes

____ 6. Antigone F. songs that comment on the action of the play or its characters

____ 7. Choragos G. the last song of the play; usually contains a moral lesson

____ 8. Teiresias H. the movement of the chorus from right to left across the stage

____ 9. Eteocles I. a prayer of thanksgiving to Dionysos at the end of the play

____ 10. Chorus J. considered a traitor to Thebes; his body was left to rot

____ 11. Eurydice K. introduces the main characters in the beginning of a play

____ 12. Episode L. the leader of the chorus

____ 13. Paean M. engaged to Antigone; son of the king

____ 14. Exodos N. the movement of the chorus from left to right across the stage

____ 15. Prologue O. he took over as the King of Thebes after the war

____ 16. Strophe P. she refused to help her sister bury Polyneices

____ 17. Antistrophe Q. ill-fated daughter of Oedipus; defied the king's decree

____ 18. Parodos R. group that sings and comments on the actions of the characters

____ 19. Tragedy S. an opening song as the chorus makes its entrance

____ 20. Ode T. a serious play in which the main character suffers from a flaw

Antigone Short Answer Unit Test 1 Page 2

II. Short Answer

1. What is King Creon's decree?

2. What news does the sentry bring to Creon? How was it decided which sentry would tell him?

3. What reason does Antigone give for defying Creon's decree?

4. What is Haimon's initial response when his father asks how he feels about the king's decision to execute Antigone?

5. What does Haimon tell King Creon about the people of Thebes' allegiance to him?

6. Who does Antigone blame for her terrible misfortune? Why?

Antigone Short Answer Unit Test 1 Page 3

7. What is the gods' reaction to Teiresias' burnt offerings? What does the prophet claim to be the cause of the gods' reaction to these offerings?

8. How has Teiresias' prophecy that Creon would pay to the gods "flesh of [his] own flesh" come true?

9. Describe what Creon saw when he looked through the crevice into Antigone's tomb.

10. Describe what happened after the messenger relayed the news about Haimon and Antigone to Eurydice.

Antigone Short Answer Unit Test 1 Page 4

III. Essay

Write a short essay about the life of Sophocles, including not only his contributions to the Greek theatre, but at least two other contributions he made in his society.

Antigone Short Answer Unit Test 1 Page 5

IV. Vocabulary

Write down the vocabulary words. Go back later and write down the correct definition for each word.

1.

2.

3.

4.

5.

6.

7.

8.

9.

10.

SHORT ANSWER UNIT TEST 1 ANSWER KEY – *Antigone*

I. Matching/Identify

J	1. Polyneices	A.	a blind prophet
O	2. Creon	B.	Oedipus' son who was buried with full honors by the state
C	3. Oedipus	C.	killed his father and married his mother; father of Antigone
P	4. Ismene	D.	a scene in a play
M	5. Haimon	E.	the queen of Thebes
Q	6. Antigone	F.	songs that comment on the action of the play or its characters
L	7. Choragos	G.	the last song of the play; usually contains a moral lesson
A	8. Teiresias	H.	the movement of the chorus from right to left across the stage
B	9. Eteocles	I.	a prayer of thanksgiving to Dionysos at the end of the play
R	10. Chorus	J.	considered a traitor to Thebes; his body was left to rot
E	11. Eurydice	K.	introduces the main characters in the beginning of a play
D	12. Episode	L.	the leader of the chorus
I	13. Paean	M.	engaged to Antigone; son of the king
G	14. Exodos	N.	the movement of the chorus from left to right across the stage
K	15. Prologue	O.	he took over as the King of Thebes after the war
H	16. Strophe	P.	she refused to help her sister bury Polyneices
N	17. Antistrophe	Q.	ill-fated daughter of Oedipus; defied the king's decree
S	18. Parodos	R.	group that sings and comments on the actions of the characters
T	19. Tragedy	S.	an opening song as the chorus makes its entrance
F	20. Ode	T.	a serious play in which the main character suffers from a flaw

Antigone Short Answer Unit Test 1 Answer Key

II. Short Answer

1. What is King Creon's decree?
   That no one should bury the dead body of Polyneices because he was a traitor to Thebes.

2. What news does the sentry bring to Creon? How was it decided which sentry would tell him?
   Someone has buried the body of Polyneices. The sentries rolled dice to see who would tell King Creon.

3. What reason does Antigone give for defying Creon's decree?
   She claims that she was fulfilling the laws of the gods by burying her brother and that the gods' laws are higher than man's laws, including Creon's.

4. What is Haimon's initial response when his father asks how he feels about the king's decision to execute Antigone?
   Haimon says that he supports and obeys his father's decisions..

5. What does Haimon tell King Creon about the people of Thebes' allegiance to him?
   Haimon tells Creon that the people only follow him out of fear of punishment, and so they say whatever he wants to hear.

6. Who does Antigone blame for her terrible misfortune? Why?
   Antigone blames her father, Oedipus, because he committed the sins of (unknowingly) killing his father and marrying his mother. Antigone is a product of that union.

7. What is the gods' reaction to Teiresias' burnt offerings? What does the prophet claim to be the cause of the gods' reaction to these offerings?
   The gods will not allow flames to come forth on the altar for the burnt offerings because the animals being sacrificed has fed off the dead body of Polyneices.

8. How has Teiresias' prophecy that Creon would pay to the gods "flesh of [his] own flesh" come true?
   Haimon kills himself after Antigone commits suicide.

9. Describe what Creon saw when he looked through the crevice into Antigone's tomb.
   Creon saw Haimon weeping over the dead body of Antigone. She had hanged herself with her own veil.

10. Describe what happened after the messenger relayed the news about Haimon and Antigone to Eurydice.
    Creon's wife, Eurydice also kills herself when she hears the news of her son's death.

Parts III and IV: For the essay portion, answers will vary. The vocabulary section will depend on which words you select from the list.

SHORT ANSWER UNIT TEST 2 - *Antigone*

I. Matching/Identify

____ 1. Polyneices   A. the movement of the chorus from right to left across the stage

____ 2. Creon   B. a scene in a play

____ 3. Oedipus   C. songs that comment on the action of the play or its characters

____ 4. Ismene   D. engaged to Antigone; son of the king

____ 5. Haimon   E. the leader of the chorus

____ 6. Antigone   F. she refused to help her sister bury Polyneices

____ 7. Choragos   G. a prayer of thanksgiving to Dionysos at the end of the play

____ 8. Teiresias   H. Oedipus' son who was buried with full honors by the state

____ 9. Eteocles   I. he took over as the King of Thebes after the war

____ 10. Chorus   J. an opening song as the chorus makes its entrance

____ 11. Eurydice   K. the movement of the chorus from left to right across the stage

____ 12. Episode   L. a serious play in which the main character suffers from a flaw

____ 13. Paean   M. ill-fated daughter of Oedipus; defied the king's decree

____ 14. Exodos   N. the last song of the play; usually contains a moral lesson

____ 15. Prologue   O. group that sings and comments on the actions of the characters

____ 16. Strophe   P. introduces the main characters in the beginning of a play

____ 17. Antistrophe   Q. a blind prophet

____ 18. Parodos   R. the queen of Thebes

____ 19. Tragedy   S. considered a traitor to Thebes; his body was left to rot

____ 20. Ode   T. killed his father and married his mother; father of Antigone

Antigone Short Answer Unit Test 2 Page 2

II. Short Answer

1. How did the new King of Thebes claim heir to the throne?

2. List man's accomplishments according to Ode 1.

3. Why is Antigone angry with Ismene?

4. Why is Creon intent on harshly punishing, even family members, all those who break the law?

5. Describe Creon's death sentence for Antigone.

Antigone Short Answer Unit Test 2 Page 3

6. What happened when the prophet began "the rites of burnt-offering at the altar"?

7. What warning does Teiresias give to King Creon if he refuses to heed the prophesies?

8. What were Creon and the messenger doing when they prayed to Hecate and Pluto?

9. Describe Haimon's reaction when Creon entered Antigone's tomb.

10. What does the Choragos claim is "always punished" by the gods?

Antigone Short Answer Unit Test 2 Page 4

III. Composition

How do various characters in *Antigone* use the rhetorical devices of logos, pathos, and ethos in an attempt to persuade other characters to accept their points of view? Give at least two examples of each type.

Antigone Short Answer Unit Test 2 Page 5

IV. Vocabulary

    Write down the vocabulary words. Go back later and write down the correct definitions for the words.

1.

2.

3.

4.

5.

6.

7.

8.

9.

10.

ANSWER KEY: SHORT ANSWER UNIT TEST 2 - *Antigone*

I. Matching/Identify

S	1. Polyneices	A.	the movement of the chorus from right to left across the stage
I	2. Creon	B.	a scene in a play
T	3. Oedipus	C.	songs that comment on the action of the play or its characters
F	4. Ismene	D.	engaged to Antigone; son of the king
D	5. Haimon	E.	the leader of the chorus
M	6. Antigone	F.	she refused to help her sister bury Polyneices
E	7. Choragos	G.	a prayer of thanksgiving to Dionysos at the end of the play
Q	8. Teiresias	H.	Oedipus' son who was buried with full honors by the state
H	9. Eteocles	I.	he took over as the King of Thebes after the war
O	10. Chorus	J.	an opening song as the chorus makes its entrance
R	11. Eurydice	K.	the movement of the chorus from left to right across the stage
B	12. Episode	L.	a serious play in which the main character suffers from a flaw
G	13. Paean	M.	ill-fated daughter of Oedipus; defied the king's decree
N	14. Exodos	N.	the last song of the play; usually contains a moral lesson
P	15. Prologue	O.	group that sings and comments on the actions of the characters
A	16. Strophe	P.	introduces the main characters in the beginning of a play
K	17. Antistrophe	Q.	a blind prophet
J	18. Parodos	R.	the queen of Thebes
L	19. Tragedy	S.	considered a traitor to Thebes; his body was left to rot
C	20. Ode	T.	killed his father and married his mother; father of Antigone

Antigone Short Answer Unit Test 2 Answer Key

II. Short Answer

1. How did the new King of Thebes claim heir to the throne?
    The former king, Oedipus, had been married to Creon's sister. When Oedipus' sons both died in the war, Creon claimed to be the next male in line for the throne.

2. List man's accomplishments according to Ode 1.
    a. *he conquered the seas*
    b. *he planted and harvested the Earth*
    c. *he has command over the creatures of the earth (birds and fish as well)*
    d. *he has created language*
    e. *he has built shelters against the elements*
    f. *he has created government*

3. Why is Antigone angry with Ismene?
    Ismene insists on being punished along with Antigone, but Antigone says that since Ismene would not help her bury their brother, Polyneices, then she has no right to share in her punishment.

4. Why is Creon intent on harshly punishing, even family members, all those who break the law?
    Creon has a shaky claim to the throne, and he is afraid of looking weak in the eyes of the people.

5. Describe Creon's death sentence for Antigone.
    He will lock her in a stone vault with enough food for a day. If she is rescued by her gods, then she may go free. But if she dies, he is absolved of any guilt from her death since she had the opportunity to get away.

6. What happened when the prophet began "the rites of burnt-offering at the altar"?
    No flames would burn on the altar, but the animals to be sacrificed melted and turned to ash. This was because the animals used in the sacrifices had eaten of the dead Polyneices and the gods were displeased.

7. What warning does Teiresias give to King Creon if he refuses to heed the prophesies?
    If Creon refuses to heed his warning, then he will be forced to pay to the gods "flesh of [his] flesh" as punishment.

8. What were Creon and the messenger doing when they prayed to Hecate and Pluto?
    They were burying the remains of Polyneices and building a barrow over his urn.

Antigone Short Answer Unit Test 2 Answer Key

9. Describe Haimon's reaction when Creon entered Antigone's tomb.
   Haimon was angered because he blamed Creon for Antigone's death. He rushed at Creon with his sword but missed. He then plunged the sword into his own side and died with Antigone in his arms.

10. What does the Choragos claim is "always punished" by the gods?
    The gods always punish "big words" (pride).

Parts III and IV:
For the essay portion, answers will vary. The vocabulary section will depend on which words you select from the list.

ADVANCED SHORT ANSWER UNIT TEST - *Antigone*

I. Matching/Identify

____ 1. logos   A. the purification of a character's emotions; an emotional release

____ 2. hubris   B. the attempt to use emotion as a means of persuasion

____ 3. catharsis   C. an opening song as the chorus makes its entrance

____ 4. harmartia   D. the movement of the chorus from right to left across the stage

____ 5. pathos   E. the attempt to use reason as a means of persuasion

____ 6. paean   F. the last song of the play; usually contains a moral lesson

____ 7. strophe   G. the attempt to appeal to one's sense of moral duty as persuasion

____ 8. ethos   H. arrogance demonstrated by a character as a result of his/her pride or passion

____ 9. parodos   I. a prayer of thanksgiving to Dionysos at the end of the play

____ 10. exodos   J. a tragic flaw in a character's personality

II. Short Answer

1. What is your initial reaction to Antigone's character based on her interaction with Ismene in the Prologue? List her positive and negative traits, using textual support as evidence.

2. Fully explain why King Creon does not want Polyneices buried.

Antigone Advanced Short Answer Unit Test Page 2

3. Discuss the playwright's use of dramatic irony throughout the tragedy.

4. What does Creon mean when he says, "An enemy is an enemy, even dead"?

5. What motivates Creon to stick to his decision regarding his decree? What is Antigone's motivation for her decision? What motivates Haimon to defend Antigone?

6. Explain the two metaphors that Haimon uses in his attempt to persuade his father to be merciful to Antigone.

Antigone Advanced Short Answer Unit Test Page 3

7. Explain the use of rhetorical devices of persuasion in the following scenes:
    a. the Prologue between Antigone and Ismene

    b. Scene 1 between King Creon and the Choragos

    c. Scene 2 between King Creon and Antigone

    d. Scene 3 between King Creon and Haimon

    e. Scene 5 between Teiresias and King Creon

8. Why is it particularly ironic that Teiresias, the prophet, is blind?

9. How does the fact that certain character refuse to appear weak affect the outcome of this play? What seems to be Sophocles' message about pride?

10. Lord Acton once said, "Absolute power corrupts absolutely." How can that statement be reflected in *Antigone*?

Antigone Advanced Short Answer Unit Test Page 3

III. Composition

Describe the structure of a Greek tragedy, and explain the function of each part of the production.

Antigone Advanced Short Answer Unit Test Page 4

IV. Vocabulary

A. Listen to the vocabulary words and write them here. Go back and write a definition for each.

1.

2.

3.

4.

5.

6.

7.

8.

9.

10.

11.

12.

B. For the following topic, include at least five of the vocabulary words in your response.

Haimon claims that the people of Thebes only follow Creon out of fear. Think of examples of others who have only gone along with something/someone because they were afraid of the consequences of NOT going along.

ADVANCED MATCHING ANSWER KEY - *Antigone*

I. Matching/Identify

E	1. logos	A.	the purification of a character's emotions; an emotional release
H	2. hubris	B.	the attempt to use emotion as a means of persuasion
A	3. catharsis	C.	an opening song as the chorus makes its entrance
J	4. harmartia	D.	the movement of the chorus from right to left across the stage
B	5. pathos	E.	the attempt to use reason as a means of persuasion
I	6. paean	F.	the last song of the play; usually contains a moral lesson
D	7. strophe	G.	the attempt to appeal to one's sense of moral duty as persuasion
G	8. ethos	H.	arrogance demonstrated by a character as a result of his/her pride or passion
C	9. parodos	I.	a prayer of thanksgiving to Dionysos at the end of the play
F	10. exodos	J.	a tragic flaw in a character's personality

MULTIPLE CHOICE UNIT TEST 1 - *Antigone*

I. Matching/Identify

____ 1. Polyneices   A. a blind prophet

____ 2. Creon   B. Oedipus' son who was buried with full honors by the state

____ 3. Oedipus   C. killed his father and married his mother; father of Antigone

____ 4. Ismene   D. a scene in a play

____ 5. Haimon   E. the queen of Thebes

____ 6. Antigone   F. songs that comment on the action of the play or its characters

____ 7. Choragos   G. the last song of the play; usually contains a moral lesson

____ 8. Teiresias   H. the movement of the chorus from right to left across the stage

____ 9. Eteocles   I. a prayer of thanksgiving to Dionysos at the end of the play

____ 10. Chorus   J. considered a traitor to Thebes; his body was left to rot

____ 11. Eurydice   K. introduces the main characters in the beginning of a play

____ 12. Episode   L. the leader of the chorus

____ 13. Paean   M. engaged to Antigone; son of the king

____ 14. Exodos   N. the movement of the chorus from left to right across the stage

____ 15. Prologue   O. he took over as the King of Thebes after the war

____ 16. Strophe   P. she refused to help her sister bury Polyneices

____ 17. Antistrophe   Q. ill-fated daughter of Oedipus; defied the king's decree

____ 18. Parodos   R. group that sings and comments on the actions of the characters

____ 19. Tragedy   S. an opening song as the chorus makes its entrance

____ 20. Ode   T. a serious play in which the main character suffers from a flaw

Antigone Multiple Choice Unit 1 Test Page 2

II. Multiple Choice

1. What is King Creon's decree?
    A. Eteocles is to be buried with honors while Polyneices is left for the birds.
    B. Polyneices is to be buried with honors while Eteocles is left for the birds.
    C. Oedipus is to be exiled from Thebes.
    D. Antigone must die for burying her brother, Eteocles.

2. How did the new King of Thebes claim heir to the throne?
    A. The former king was his father.
    B. The former king was his brother-in-law whose sons both died in battle.
    C. The former king was his uncle.
    D. The former king left no heir, so Creon simply took the empty throne.

3. What news does the sentry bring to Creon?
    A. Polyneices is dead.
    B. The people of Thebes are preparing to riot because of the king's decree.
    C. Someone has gone against the king's decree and buried Polyneices.
    D. Someone has removed the body of Polyneices from the field where it had been left.

4. Which of the following is not one of man's accomplishments according to Ode 1?
    A. He has created government.
    B. He has conquered the seas.
    C. He has created roads to reach far lands.
    D. He has created language.

5. What reason does Antigone give for defying Creon's decree?
    A. She had not heard the decree.
    B. She was trying to get back at Creon for taking the crown of Thebes.
    C. Ismene forced her to do it against her will.
    D. God's laws demand burial and they are more important than man's laws.

6. Why is Antigone angry with Ismene?
    A. Ismene planned to share in Antigone's punishment, but would not help her.
    B. Ismene told the sentries that Antigone had buried Polyneices.
    C. Ismene told Creon what Antigone had planned.
    D. Ismene refuses to acknowledge Antigone as her sister.

7. What is Haimon's initial response when his father asks how he feels about the king's decision to execute Antigone?
    A. He is outraged that his father would execute his own niece.
    B. He falls to he knees and begs his father to kill him in her place.
    C. He tells his father that he supports and obeys his father's decisions.
    D. He agrees that Antigone should be executed for her crime against the state.

Antigone Multiple Choice Unit 1 Test   Page 3

8. Which of the following is not one of the reasons why Creon is intent on harshly punishing, even family members, all those who break the law?
    A. He believes that his people will not respect him as king if he shows leniency.
    B. He is afraid of appearing weak in the eyes of his people.
    C. He wants to make an example of Antigone to demonstrate his power.
    D. He is an envious man who would never relinquish the throne under anyone.

9. What does Haimon tell King Creon about the people of Thebes' allegiance to him?
    A. He says that they are willing to defend him from any opponents.
    B. He says that the people have no respect for Creon and ridicule him behind his back.
    C. He says that the people only follow Creon out of fear and say what Creon wants to hear.
    D. He says that the people are prepared to revolt if Creon does not free Antigone.

10. Describe Creon's death sentence for Antigone.
    A. She will be hanged by the neck until dead.
    B. She will be shot at dawn.
    C. She will be locked in a stone tomb with only enough food for one day and left to die.
    D. She will be publicly stoned to death.

11. Who does Antigone blame for her terrible misfortune?
    A. Creon
    B. Polyneices
    C. Oedipus
    D. Haimon

12. What happened when the prophet began "the rites of burnt-offering at the altar"?
    A. The flames instantly turned all to white ash.
    B. The animal's body exploded in Teiresias' face.
    C. There was no flame, but the sacrifice melted on the altar.
    D. The gods accepted the offering.

13. What does the prophet claim to be the cause of the gods' reaction to their offerings?
    A. They are angry that Antigone defied Creon.
    B. They are angry that Creon refuses to pay homage to the gods in any way.
    C. They are angry regarding Creaon's treatment of Polyneices and Antigone.
    D. Antigone must pay for the sins of her father, Oedipus.

14. What warning does Teiresias give to King Creon if he refuses to heed the prophesies?
    A. Creon will die.
    B. The king will lose what is dear to him in repayment to the gods.
    C. Antigone will haunt his dreams forever.
    D. The city of Thebes will rise against him and revolt.

Antigone Multiple Choice Unit 1 Test   Page 4

15. How has Teiresias' prophecy that Creon would pay to the gods "flesh of [his] own flesh" come true?
    A. Creon was forced to yield a pound of flesh as a burnt-offering.
    B. Creon's only daughter was struck down by the gods in vengeance for Antigone.
    C. Creon's son has killed himself.
    D. Creon's lineage is cursed by the gods for twenty generations.

16. What were Creon and the messenger doing when they prayed to Hecate and Pluto?
    A. begging the gods to remove the curse from Creon's family
    B. burying Polyneices
    C. freeing Antigone
    D. praying to restore Polyneices to life

17. Describe what Creon saw when he looked through the crevice into Antigone's tomb.
    A. Antigone's body was hanging from the ceiling by her own veil.
    B. Haimon was weeping over the dead body of Antigone.
    C. Haimon was rescuing Antigone from the tomb; they were running away.
    D. Antigone was praying to the gods for help.

18. Describe Haimon's reaction when Creon entered Antigone's tomb.
    A. He put Antigone's dead body at Creon's feet.
    B. He ran in fear of being accused of treason.
    C. He attacked Creon.
    D. He wept in his father's arms.

19. What happened after the messenger relayed the news about Haimon and Antigone to Eurydice?
    A. She made a sacrifice of thanks to Zeus.
    B. She killed Creon.
    C. She rejoiced that Haimon and Antigone were finally together.
    D. She killed herself.

20. What does the Choragos claim is "always punished" by the gods?
    A. greed
    B. lust
    C. big words
    D. treason

Antigone Multiple Choice Unit 1 Test Page 5

III. Composition

1. What is your initial reaction to Antigone's character based on her interaction with Ismene in the Prologue? List her positive and negative traits, using textual support as evidence.

2 Discuss the playwright's use of dramatic irony throughout the tragedy.

3. What motivates Creon to stick to his decision regarding his decree? What is Antigone's motivation for her decision? What motivates Haimon to defend Antigone?

4. Why is it particularly ironic that Teiresias, the prophet, is blind?

5. How does the fact that certain character refuse to appear weak affect the outcome of this play? What seems to be Sophocles' message about pride?

Antigone Multiple Choice Unit 1 Test Page 6

IV. Vocabulary - Match the correct definitions to the words.

____ 1. decree   A. to walk or conduct oneself with an insolent or arrogant air

____ 2. yield   B. having the capacity to exert a strong, irresistible force on

____ 3. roused   C. to commit an offense by violating a law or command; sin

____ 4. sated   D. an authoritative order having the force of law

____ 5. swagger   E. righteousness by virtue of being pious

____ 6. demoralizing   F. to undermine the confidence or morale of; dishearten

____ 7. prow   G. to give up (an advantage, for example) to another; concede

____ 8. defy   H. in a deplorable state of distress or misfortune; miserable

____ 9. compulsive   I. the internal organs, especially the intestines

____ 10. embers   J. a noisy quarrel or fight

____ 11. diviners   K. satisfied to excess

____ 12. brawl   L. to refuse to submit to or cooperate with

____ 13. piety   M. inclined to be lenient or merciful

____ 14. vile   N. deserving of contempt or scorn; evil

____ 15. wretched   O. small, glowing pieces of coal or wood, as in a dying fire

____ 16. lamentation   P. very strong winds

____ 17. transgress   Q. excited, as to anger or action; stirred up

____ 18. gales   R. a cry of sorrow and grief

____ 19. entrails   S. the forward part of a ship's hull

____ 20. clement   T. those who can predict the future; fortune-tellers

MULTIPLE CHOICE UNIT TEST 2 - *Antigone*

I. Matching

____ 1. Polyneices   A. the movement of the chorus from right to left across the stage

____ 2. Creon   B. a scene in a play

____ 3. Oedipus   C. songs that comment on the action of the play or its characters

____ 4. Ismene   D. engaged to Antigone; son of the king

____ 5. Haimon   E. the leader of the chorus

____ 6. Antigone   F. she refused to help her sister bury Polyneices

____ 7. Choragos   G. a prayer of thanksgiving to Dionysos at the end of the play

____ 8. Teiresias   H. Oedipus' son who was buried with full honors by the state

____ 9. Eteocles   I. he took over as the King of Thebes after the war

____ 10. Chorus   J. an opening song as the chorus makes its entrance

____ 11. Eurydice   K. the movement of the chorus from left to right across the stage

____ 12. Episode   L. a serious play in which the main character suffers from a flaw

____ 13. Paean   M. ill-fated daughter of Oedipus; defied the king's decree

____ 14. Exodos   N. the last song of the play; usually contains a moral lesson

____ 15. Prologue   O. group that sings and comments on the actions of the characters

____ 16. Strophe   P. introduces the main characters in the beginning of a play

____ 17. Antistrophe   Q. a blind prophet

____ 18. Parodos   R. the queen of Thebes

____ 19. Tragedy   S. considered a traitor to Thebes; his body was left to rot

____ 20. Ode   T. killed his father and married his mother; father of Antigone

Antigone Multiple Choice Unit 2 Test Page 2

II. Multiple Choice

1. How are Antigone and Ismene related?
    A. They are cousins.
    B. Antigone is Ismene's daughter.
    C. They are sisters.
    D. Ismene is Antigone's daughter.

2. What is Ismene's decision regarding the King's decree?
    A. She agrees with Antigone and they bury Eteocles.
    B. She is afraid to go against the king, so she refuses to help her sister.
    C. She agrees with Antigone and they bury Polyneices.
    D. She plans to tell the king about Antigone's decision.

3. According to the Choragos, what does God hate?
    A. a liar
    B. a murderer
    C. a braggart
    D. a thief

4. What crime has Ployneices committed in the opinion of the king?
    A. murder
    B. treason
    C. theft
    D. adultery

5. How does Creon believe the act of burying Polyneices was carried out?
    A. The king's known political enemies crept onto the field at night.
    B. One of the guards must have moved the body and handed it over to the priests.
    C. Polyneices' wife paid the sentries to allow her to bury her husband.
    D. The sentries had been bribed by the king's enemies and they buried the body.

6. According to Ode 1, what is the most wonderful of all the world's wonders?
    A. the stormgray sea
    B. man
    C. the lightbones birds and beasts
    D. the lion on a hill

7. How did the guards manage to capture Antigone?
    A. They removed the dirt from Polyneices' body and waited to see who came back.
    B. Ismene told the sentries where to find her.
    C. When she was going back to the body, she tripped, making a large noise.
    D. They didn't capture her; she turned herself in.

Antigone Multiple Choice Unit 2 Test   Page 3

8. Besides being Antigone's uncle, how else are Creon and Antigone related?
    A. They are cousins.
    B. Antigone is the mother of his child.
    C. Creon and Antigone are both siblings to Oedipus.
    D. Antigone is engaged to Creon's son.

9. What does Creon say that men pray for?
    A. loyal wives
    B. dutiful sons
    C. subordinates who follow orders unquestioningly
    D. the strength to do what is right and pleasing in God's eyes

10. How does the city feel about Antigone's crime?
    A. They do not view it as a crime, but as a loving sister caring for her dead brother.
    B. They want Creon to execute her publicly.
    C. They believe that Antigone's body should suffer that same fate decreed to Polyneices'.
    D. They believe that Antigone should be merely banished and not executed.

11. What does Creon sarcastically say would have man singing forever?
    A. lewd women
    B. their own pride
    C. their greed
    D. if death could be postponed by singing

12. What is the "half remembered tale of horror" that old men tell?
    A. A young girl is chained to a rock to await a terrible monster.
    B. A man was wandering in a labyrinth to seek out the Minotaur.
    C. A king's mistress tore out the eyes of his sons in a jealous rage.
    D. Young men gazed at Medusa and were instantly turned to stone.

13. Who is the blind prophet who comes to speak to King Creon?
    A. Oedipus
    B. Eurydice
    C. Choragos
    D. Teiresias

14. What does the prophet claim to be the cause of the gods' reaction to their offerings?
    A. They are angry that Antigone defied Creon.
    B. They are angry that Creon refuses to pay homage to the gods in any way.
    C. They are angry regarding Creaon's treatment of Polyneices and Antigone.
    D. Antigone must pay for the sins of her father, Oedipus.

Antigone Multiple Choice Unit 2 Test Page 4

15. What does the prophet claim can be done to repair the evil performed against the gods?
    A. Antigone should beg mercy of Creon.
    B. Creon should admit his errors and put them right.
    C. Creon can offer a sacrifice on the altar of Zeus to atone for his sins.
    D. Antigone can publicly apologize for defying Creon's decree.

16. What is King Creon's reaction to Teiresias' message?
    A. He angrily refuses to yield because he does not want to appear weak.
    B. He believes that Teiresias is lying to him and that he is no prophet.
    C. He is glad that the gods will relent if Antigone apologizes.
    D. He repents his errors and tries to make amends.

17. Who does the messenger claim is "a walking dead man"?
    A. Polyneices
    B. Creon
    C. Teiresias
    D. Oedipus

18. Who is Eurydice?
    A. Creon's wife
    B. Antigone's sister
    C. Creon's only daughter
    D. Antigone's mother

19. Describe Haimon's reaction when Creon entered Antigone's tomb.
    A. He put Antigone's dead body at Creon's feet.
    B. He ran in fear of being accused of treason.
    C. He attacked Creon.
    D. He wept in his father's arms.

20. What does the Choragos claim is "always punished" by the gods?
    A. greed
    B. lust
    C. big words
    D. treason

Antigone Multiple Choice Unit 2 Test Page 5

III. Composition

1. Fully explain why King Creon does not want Polyneices buried.

2. What does Creon mean when he says, "An enemy is an enemy, even dead"?

3. Explain the two metaphors that Haimon uses in his attempt to persuade his father to be merciful to Antigone.

4. Lord Acton once said, "Absolute power corrupts absolutely." How can that statement be reflected in *Antigone*?

5. What is your initial reaction to Creon's character based on his "state of the union address" in scene 1? List his positive and negative traits, using textual support as evidence.

Antigone Multiple Choice Unit 2 Test Page 6

IV. Vocabulary - Match the correct definitions to the words.

____ 1. carrion   A. to be half-asleep

____ 2. eddy   B. an event that brings terrible loss; disaster

____ 3. bray   C. a fortress in a commanding position in or near a city

____ 4. sultry   D. a large mound of earth or stones placed over a burial site

____ 5. deflects   E. a formal command

____ 6. endured   F. a watch kept during normal sleeping hours

____ 7. edict   G. to fill beyond capacity, especially with food

____ 8. drowse   H. made of brass

____ 9. perverse   I. a current of water moving against the main current

____ 10. vigil   J. without civilizing influences

____ 11. slacken   K. a loud, harsh sound resembling that of a donkey

____ 12. tormented   L. to be greater in strength or influence; triumph

____ 13. brazen   M. very humid and hot

____ 14. prevail   N. persisting in an error or fault; wrongly self-willed or stubborn

____ 15. calamity   O. bore with tolerance

____ 16. glut   P. feeding on dead and decaying flesh

____ 17. folly   Q. a lack of good sense, understanding, or foresight

____ 18. citadel   R. to make or become less tense, taut, or firm; loosen

____ 19. barbaric   S. turns aside or cause to turn aside

____ 20. barrow   T. caused great physical pain or mental anguish

ANSWER SHEET - *Antigone*
Multiple Choice Unit Tests

I. Matching	II. Multiple Choice	IV. Vocabulary
1. ___	1. ___	1. ___
2. ___	2. ___	2. ___
3. ___	3. ___	3. ___
4. ___	4. ___	4. ___
5. ___	5. ___	5. ___
6. ___	6. ___	6. ___
7. ___	7. ___	7. ___
8. ___	8. ___	8. ___
9. ___	9. ___	9. ___
10. ___	10. ___	10. ___
11. ___	11. ___	11. ___
12. ___	12. ___	12. ___
13. ___	13. ___	13. ___
14. ___	14. ___	14. ___
15. ___	15. ___	15. ___
16. ___	16. ___	16. ___
17. ___	17. ___	17. ___
18. ___	18. ___	18. ___
19. ___	19. ___	19. ___
20. ___	20. ___	20. ___

ANSWER KEY - *Antigone*
Multiple Choice Unit Test 1

I. Matching	II. Multiple Choice	IV. Vocabulary
1. J	1. A	1. D
2. O	2. B	2. G
3. C	3. C	3. Q
4. P	4. C	4. K
5. M	5. D	5. A
6. Q	6. A	6. F
7. L	7. C	7. S
8. A	8. D	8. L
9. B	9. C	9. B
10. R	10. C	10. O
11. E	11. C	11. T
12. D	12. C	12. J
13. I	13. C	13. E
14. G	14. B	14. N
15. K	15. C	15. H
16. H	16. B	16. R
17. N	17. B	17. C
18. S	18. C	18. P
19. T	19. D	19. I
20. F	20. C	20. M

Part III: Answers will vary

ANSWER KEY - *Antigone*
Multiple Choice Unit Test 2

I. Matching	II. Multiple Choice	IV. Vocabulary
1. S	1. C	1. P
2. I	2. B	2. I
3. T	3. C	3. K
4. F	4. B	4. M
5. D	5. D	5. S
6. M	6. B	6. O
7. E	7. A	7. E
8. Q	8. D	8. A
9. H	9. B	9. N
10. O	10. A	10. F
11. R	11. D	11. R
12. B	12. C	12. T
13. G	13. D	13. H
14. N	14. C	14. L
15. P	15. B	15. B
16. A	16. A	16. G
17. K	17. B	17. Q
18. J	18. A	18. C
19. L	19. C	19. J
20. C	20. C	20. D

Part III: Answers will vary

UNIT RESOURCE MATERIALS

BULLETIN BOARD IDEAS - *Antigone*

1. Save one corner of the board for the best of students' *Antigone* writing assignments.

2. Take one of the word search puzzles from the extra activities packet and with a marker copy it over in a large size on the bulletin board. Write the clue words to find to one side. Invite students prior to and after class to find the words and circle them on the bulletin board.

3. Write several of the most significant quotations from the book onto the board on brightly colored paper.

4. Make a bulletin board listing the vocabulary words for this unit. As you complete sections of the play and discuss the vocabulary for each section, write the definitions on the bulletin board. (If your board is one students face frequently, it will help them learn the words.)

5. Create a bulletin board depicting the history of Greek Theatre.

6. Devote an entire bulletin board to Sophocles and his life.

7. Create bulletin boards surrounding the mythological tragedies completed by the students.

8. Decorate a bulletin board with masks created by the students.

9. Display the characterization posters completed by the students.

10. Display the odes created by the students.

11. Create an outline of the structure of a Greek tragedy.

12. Create a bulletin board for the story of Oedipus that forms the background of this tragedy.

13. Create a bulletin board devoted to those who stood up against tyranny.

14. Take pictures as the students perform (either from *Antigone* or from their own tragedies) and display them on a bulletin board.

15. Devote a bulletin board to various moral dilemmas and call it "What Would YOU Do?"

EXTRA ACTIVITIES - *Antigone*

One of the difficulties in teaching a novel is that all students don't read at the same speed. One student who likes to read may take the book home and finish it in a day or two. Sometimes a few students finish the in-class assignments early. The problem, then, is finding suitable extra activities for students.

One thing that seems to help is to keep a little library in the classroom. For this unit on *Antigone*, you might check out from the school library *Oedipus Rex, Oedipus at Colonus,* and a collection of Greek myths.. Any stories or articles about Sophocles, Greek culture (especially burial practices), Greek theatre (or theatre in general, for comparisons/contrasts), or the society of Ancient Greece would also be of interest.

Other things you may keep on hand are puzzles. We have made some relating directly to *Antigone* for you. Feel free to duplicate them for your students to use. We also offer Puzzle Packs --complete manuals of puzzles and games related to the play, sold separately.

Some students may like to draw. You might devise a contest or allow some extra-credit grade for students who draw characters or scenes from *Antigone.* Note, too, that if the students do not want to keep their drawings you may pick up some extra bulletin board materials this way. If you have a contest and you supply the prize (a CD or something like that perhaps), you could, possibly, make the drawing itself a non-returnable entry fee.

The pages which follow contain games, puzzles and worksheets. The keys, when appropriate, immediately follow the puzzle or worksheet. There are two main groups of activities: one group for the unit; that is, generally relating to *Antigone* text, and another group of activities related strictly to *Antigone* vocabulary.

Directions for these games, puzzles and worksheets are self-explanatory. The object here is to provide you with extra materials you may use in any way you choose.

Have students work together to make a time line chronology of the events in the story. Take a large piece of construction paper and on one wall (or however you can physically arrange it in your room) and make the events of the story along it. Students may want to add drawings or cut-out pictures to represent the events (as well as a written statement).

Have students design a book cover (front and back and inside flaps) for *Antigone*.

Antigone Word List

No.	Word	Clue/Definition
1.	AESCHYLUS	Greek playwright who was defeated in the tetralogy competition by Sophocles
2.	ANTIGONE	Ill-fated daughter of Oedipus; defied the king's decree
3.	ANTISTROPHE	Movement of the chorus from left to right across the stage
4.	BATTLE	Oedipus's 2 sons were killed in ___.
5.	BIRDS	Teiresias heard these & they frightened him.
6.	BURY	Creon decreed it illegal to ___ Polyneices.
7.	CATHARSIS	Purification of a character's emotions; an emotional release
8.	CHORAGOS	Leader of the chorus
9.	CHORUS	Group that sings and comments on the actions of the characters
10.	CREON	Took over as King of Thebes after the war
11.	DEATH	Penalty for burying Polyneices
12.	DIONYSIA	Festival honoring the Greek God of wine
13.	DIONYSOS	God of wine in whose honor Greek tragedies were performed
14.	EPISODE	Scene in a play
15.	ETEOCLES	Oedipus's son buried with full honors
16.	ETHOS	Attempt to appeal to one's sense of moral duty as persuasion
17.	EURYDICE	Queen of Thebes
18.	EXODUS	Last song of the play; usually contains a moral lesson
19.	GOD	The fortunate man is one who has never tasted ___'s vengeance.
20.	GOLD	According to Creon, all prophets love this.
21.	HAIMON	Engaged to Antigone; son of Creon
22.	HARMARTIA	Tragic flaw in a character's personality
23.	HUBRIS	Arrogance demonstrated by a character as a result of his/her pride or passion
24.	ISMENE	Refused to help her sister bury Polyneices
25.	LANGUAGE	One of man's accomplishments: he created ___
26.	LOGOS	Attempt to use reason as a means of persuasion
27.	LOVE	Even the pure Immortals cannot escape it.
28.	MAN	___ is the most wonderful of all the world's wonders.
29.	ODES	Songs that comment on the action of the play or its characters
30.	OEDIPUS	Killed his father & married his mother; father of Antigone
31.	PAEAN	Prayer of thanksgiving to Dionysos at the end of the play
32.	PARADOS	Opening song as the chorus makes its entrance
33.	PATHOS	Attempt to use emotion as a means of persuasion
34.	POLYNEICES	Considered a traitor to Thebes; his body was left to rot
35.	PROLOGUE	Introduces the main characters at the beginning of the play
36.	REASON	God's crowning gift to man, according to Haimon
37.	SATYR	Play that comically portrayed mythological stories or poked fun at politics
38.	SEAS	One of man's accomplishments: he conquered the ___
39.	SISTERS	Relationship between Antigone and Ismene
40.	SOPHOCLES	Author of the play Antigone
41.	SOUL	When his body was buried, Polyneices's ___ could move to the Underworld.
42.	STROPHE	Movement of the chorus from right to left across the stage
43.	TEIRESIAS	Blind prophet
44.	TETRAOLOGY	Collection of plays submitted in the Dionysia competition
45.	THEBES	It has seven gates in a yawning ring.
46.	THESPIS	Considered to be the Father of Greek Theater
47.	TRAGEDY	Serious play in which the main character suffers from a flaw
48.	ZEUS	Those who anger him will suffer his wrath.

WORD SEARCH Antigone

```
H A R M A R T I A O E D I P U S S M E L
Z J G M H K P R V B L C R R J F R H S V
Y D N Y W V H E D O S I P E Y L P H G D
V D Y Z A H M F G Z S S E L C O E T E W
P O L Y N E I C E S N V E U R Y D I C E
N F C X T F M L F S Q D B T V K I M L Y
T L K B I M X T S J T R S W F X O V V M
P R N J G R K A E M I N D S F N X D V
G W A D O M I W S T T S W O D T Y J Y H
O H D G N S B S Q N R N G B R S S S Z F
D C C R E O N C A T H A R S I S O G O L
O D J R C D R Q J T R M O J B D S T S G
C D I W H T Y P E O Y I W L A V S H S Y
E E E X O Y N V H R S R H R O E U E I C
T X C S R W O C Z M A N A S S G L B S G
N Y O U U L S P E T I P I O T A Y E T J
D R B D S H A N U M S S M U R U H S E M
M R E D U Z E F S S Y O O L O G C P R D
P A T H O S R N I R N P N B P N S R S D
B N H Y P Z A P R W O H S A H A E O E H
D L O H P E S M B R I O X T E L A L A W
F E S G A E X W U D D C W T J B Y O S W
Q T A P H B M N H J C L Z L B Y W G V R
W J L T T F Y X F X L E B E M S L U H V
G B P T H F W H B X S S X H S M H E Z J
```

AESCHYLUS	DEATH	HAIMON	PAEAN	SOUL
ANTIGONE	DIONYSIA	HARMARTIA	PARADOS	STROPHE
ANTISTROPHE	DIONYSOS	HUBRIS	PATHOS	TEIRESIAS
BATTLE	EPISODE	ISMENE	POLYNEICES	TETRAOLOGY
BIRDS	ETEOCLES	LANGUAGE	PROLOGUE	THEBES
BURY	ETHOS	LOGOS	REASON	THESPIS
CATHARSIS	EURYDICE	LOVE	SATYR	TRAGEDY
CHORAGOS	EXODUS	MAN	SEAS	ZEUS
CHORUS	GOD	ODES	SISTERS	
CREON	GOLD	OEDIPUS	SOPHOCLES	

WORD SEARCH ANSWER KEY Antigone

AESCHYLUS	DEATH	HAIMON	PAEAN	SOUL
ANTIGONE	DIONYSIA	HARMARTIA	PARADOS	STROPHE
ANTISTROPHE	DIONYSOS	HUBRIS	PATHOS	TEIRESIAS
BATTLE	EPISODE	ISMENE	POLYNEICES	TETRAOLOGY
BIRDS	ETEOCLES	LANGUAGE	PROLOGUE	THEBES
BURY	ETHOS	LOGOS	REASON	THESPIS
CATHARSIS	EURYDICE	LOVE	SATYR	TRAGEDY
CHORAGOS	EXODUS	MAN	SEAS	ZEUS
CHORUS	GOD	ODES	SISTERS	
CREON	GOLD	OEDIPUS	SOPHOCLES	

CROSSWORD Antigone

Across
1. Penalty for burying Polyneices
2. Engaged to Antigone; son of Creon
6. Killed his father & married his mother; father of Antigone
9. It has seven gates in a yawning ring.
10. Scene in a play
11. Relationship between Antigone and Ismene
14. Songs that comment on the action of the play or its characters
15. ___ is the most wonderful of all the world's wonders.
18. Refused to help her sister bury Polyneices
20. Introduces the main characters at the beginning of the play
21. Took over as King of Thebes after the war
22. The fortunate man is one who has never tasted ___'s vengeance.
23. Considered a traitor to Thebes; his body was left to rot

Down
1. Festival honoring the Greek God of wine
3. Ill-fated daughter of Oedipus; defied the king's decree
4. Prayer of thanksgiving to Dionysos at the end of the play
5. Those who anger him will suffer his wrath.
7. One of man's accomplishments: he conquered the ___
8. Author of the play Antigone
9. Blind prophet
12. Play that comically portrayed mythological stories or poked fun at politics
13. God's crowning gift to man, according to Haimon
16. Greek playwright who was defeated in the tetralogy competition by Sophocles
17. Creon decreed it illegal to ___ Polyneices.
19. Queen of Thebes
20. Opening song as the chorus makes its entrance
22. According to Creon, all prophets love this.

CROSSWORD ANSWER KEY Antigone

¹D	E	A	T	H		²H	³A	I	M	O	N		⁴P
I							N				⁵Z		A
⁶O	E	D	I	P	⁷U	S		⁸S	⁹T	H	E	B	E	S
N					¹⁰E	P	I	S	O	D	E		U		A
Y					A		G		P		I		S		N
¹¹S	¹²I	S	¹³T	E	R	S		O		H		R			
I		A		E			N		¹⁴O	D	E	S			
A		T		¹⁵M	A	N		E		C		S			¹⁶A
		Y		S		¹⁷B		L		¹⁸I	S	M	¹⁹E	N	E
	²⁰P	R	O	L	O	G	U	E		E		A		U		S
	A			N		R		S		S			R		C
²¹C	R	E	O	N		Y							Y		H
	A								²²G	O	D			Y
	D								O		I			L
²³P	O	L	Y	N	E	I	C	E	S		L		C		U
	S								L		D	E		S

Across
1. Penalty for burying Polyneices
2. Engaged to Antigone; son of Creon
6. Killed his father & married his mother; father of Antigone
9. It has seven gates in a yawning ring.
10. Scene in a play
11. Relationship between Antigone and Ismene
14. Songs that comment on the action of the play or its characters
15. ___ is the most wonderful of all the world's wonders.
18. Refused to help her sister bury Polyneices
20. Introduces the main characters at the beginning of the play
21. Took over as King of Thebes after the war
22. The fortunate man is one who has never tasted ___'s vengeance.
23. Considered a traitor to Thebes; his body was left to rot

Down
1. Festival honoring the Greek God of wine
3. Ill-fated daughter of Oedipus; defied the king's decree
4. Prayer of thanksgiving to Dionysos at the end of the play
5. Those who anger him will suffer his wrath.
7. One of man's accomplishments: he conquered the ___
8. Author of the play Antigone
9. Blind prophet
12. Play that comically portrayed mythological stories or poked fun at politics
13. God's crowning gift to man, according to Haimon
16. Greek playwright who was defeated in the tetralogy competition by Sophocles
17. Creon decreed it illegal to ___ Polyneices.
19. Queen of Thebes
20. Opening song as the chorus makes its entrance
22. According to Creon, all prophets love this.

MATCHING 1 Antigone

___ 1. TETRAOLOGY   A. Refused to help her sister bury Polyneices

___ 2. EURYDICE   B. Attempt to use reason as a means of persuasion

___ 3. EXODUS   C. Opening song as the chorus makes its entrance

___ 4. SATYR   D. Attempt to appeal to one's sense of moral duty as persuasion

___ 5. LANGUAGE   E. Took over as King of Thebes after the war

___ 6. LOGOS   F. Queen of Thebes

___ 7. CREON   G. Collection of plays submitted in the Dionysia competition

___ 8. BURY   H. One of man's accomplishments: he created ___

___ 9. ZEUS   I. Greek playwright who was defeated in the tetralogy competition by Sophocles

___ 10. BATTLE   J. Teiresias heard these & they frightened him.

___ 11. BIRDS   K. Attempt to use emotion as a means of persuasion

___ 12. PATHOS   L. Purification of a character's emotions; an emotional release

___ 13. CHORAGOS   M. Author of the play Antigone

___ 14. ETHOS   N. Oedipus's 2 sons were killed in ___.

___ 15. DEATH   O. ___ is the most wonderful of all the world's wonders.

___ 16. MAN   P. Scene in a play

___ 17. ODES   Q. Those who anger him will suffer his wrath.

___ 18. SOPHOCLES   R. Creon decreed it illegal to ___ Polyneices.

___ 19. PARADOS   S. Last song of the play; usually contains a moral lesson

___ 20. THESPIS   T. Leader of the chorus

___ 21. CATHARSIS   U. Penalty for burying Polyneices

___ 22. ISMENE   V. Songs that comment on the action of the play or its characters

___ 23. EPISODE   W. Considered to be the Father of Greek Theater

___ 24. ANTIGONE   X. Ill-fated daughter of Oedipus; defied the king's decree

___ 25. AESCHYLUS   Y. Play that comically portrayed mythological stories or poked fun at politics

MATCHING 1 ANSWER KEY Antigone

G - 1.	TETRAOLOGY	A.	Refused to help her sister bury Polyneices
F - 2.	EURYDICE	B.	Attempt to use reason as a means of persuasion
S - 3.	EXODUS	C.	Opening song as the chorus makes its entrance
Y - 4.	SATYR	D.	Attempt to appeal to one's sense of moral duty as persuasion
H - 5.	LANGUAGE	E.	Took over as King of Thebes after the war
B - 6.	LOGOS	F.	Queen of Thebes
E - 7.	CREON	G.	Collection of plays submitted in the Dionysia competition
R - 8.	BURY	H.	One of man's accomplishments: he created ___
Q - 9.	ZEUS	I.	Greek playwright who was defeated in the tetralogy competition by Sophocles
N - 10.	BATTLE	J.	Teiresias heard these & they frightened him.
J - 11.	BIRDS	K.	Attempt to use emotion as a means of persuasion
K - 12.	PATHOS	L.	Purification of a character's emotions; an emotional release
T - 13.	CHORAGOS	M.	Author of the play Antigone
D - 14.	ETHOS	N.	Oedipus's 2 sons were killed in ___.
U - 15.	DEATH	O.	___ is the most wonderful of all the world's wonders.
O - 16.	MAN	P.	Scene in a play
V - 17.	ODES	Q.	Those who anger him will suffer his wrath.
M - 18.	SOPHOCLES	R.	Creon decreed it illegal to ___ Polyneices.
C - 19.	PARADOS	S.	Last song of the play; usually contains a moral lesson
W - 20.	THESPIS	T.	Leader of the chorus
L - 21.	CATHARSIS	U.	Penalty for burying Polyneices
A - 22.	ISMENE	V.	Songs that comment on the action of the play or its characters
P - 23.	EPISODE	W.	Considered to be the Father of Greek Theater
X - 24.	ANTIGONE	X.	Ill-fated daughter of Oedipus; defied the king's decree
I - 25.	AESCHYLUS	Y.	Play that comically portrayed mythological stories or poked fun at politics

MATCHING 2 Antigone

___ 1. OEDIPUS A. According to Creon, all prophets love this.
___ 2. SATYR B. Those who anger him will suffer his wrath.
___ 3. ZEUS C. Attempt to appeal to one's sense of moral duty as persuasion
___ 4. EURYDICE D. Songs that comment on the action of the play or its characters
___ 5. TRAGEDY E. When his body was buried, Polyneices's ___ could move to the Underworld.
___ 6. SOPHOCLES F. Engaged to Antigone; son of Creon
___ 7. AESCHYLUS G. One of man's accomplishments: he created ___
___ 8. GOLD H. Teiresias heard these & they frightened him.
___ 9. CHORAGOS I. Oedipus's son buried with full honors
___10. ANTISTROPHE J. Killed his father & married his mother; father of Antigone
___11. PAEAN K. Greek playwright who was defeated in the tetralogy competition by Sophocles
___12. REASON L. Considered a traitor to Thebes; his body was left to rot
___13. DIONYSOS M. Serious play in which the main character suffers from a flaw
___14. LOVE N. Oedipus's 2 sons were killed in ___.
___15. ETHOS O. God of wine in whose honor Greek tragedies were performed
___16. BATTLE P. Movement of the chorus from left to right across the stage
___17. MAN Q. Creon decreed it illegal to ___ Polyneices.
___18. ETEOCLES R. Queen of Thebes
___19. BIRDS S. God's crowning gift to man, according to Haimon
___20. BURY T. Leader of the chorus
___21. SOUL U. Prayer of thanksgiving to Dionysos at the end of the play
___22. HAIMON V. Play that comically portrayed mythological stories or poked fun at politics
___23. POLYNEICES W. Author of the play Antigone
___24. ODES X. Even the pure Immortals cannot escape it.
___25. LANGUAGE Y. ___ is the most wonderful of all the world's wonders.

MATCHING 2 ANSWER KEY Antigone

J - 1. OEDIPUS		A. According to Creon, all prophets love this.
V - 2. SATYR		B. Those who anger him will suffer his wrath.
B - 3. ZEUS		C. Attempt to appeal to one's sense of moral duty as persuasion
R - 4. EURYDICE		D. Songs that comment on the action of the play or its characters
M - 5. TRAGEDY		E. When his body was buried, Polyneices's ___ could move to the Underworld.
W - 6. SOPHOCLES		F. Engaged to Antigone; son of Creon
K - 7. AESCHYLUS		G. One of man's accomplishments: he created ___
A - 8. GOLD		H. Teiresias heard these & they frightened him.
T - 9. CHORAGOS		I. Oedipus's son buried with full honors
P - 10. ANTISTROPHE		J. Killed his father & married his mother; father of Antigone
U - 11. PAEAN		K. Greek playwright who was defeated in the tetralogy competition by Sophocles
S - 12. REASON		L. Considered a traitor to Thebes; his body was left to rot
O - 13. DIONYSOS		M. Serious play in which the main character suffers from a flaw
X - 14. LOVE		N. Oedipus's 2 sons were killed in ___.
C - 15. ETHOS		O. God of wine in whose honor Greek tragedies were performed
N - 16. BATTLE		P. Movement of the chorus from left to right across the stage
Y - 17. MAN		Q. Creon decreed it illegal to ___ Polyneices.
I - 18. ETEOCLES		R. Queen of Thebes
H - 19. BIRDS		S. God's crowning gift to man, according to Haimon
Q - 20. BURY		T. Leader of the chorus
E - 21. SOUL		U. Prayer of thanksgiving to Dionysos at the end of the play
F - 22. HAIMON		V. Play that comically portrayed mythological stories or poked fun at politics
L - 23. POLYNEICES		W. Author of the play Antigone
D - 24. ODES		X. Even the pure Immortals cannot escape it.
G - 25. LANGUAGE		Y. ___ is the most wonderful of all the world's wonders.

JUGGLE LETTERS Antigone

1. TAYSR = 1. _____
Play that comically portrayed mythological stories or poked fun at politics

2. YLSHUCSAE = 2. _____
Greek playwright who was defeated in the tetralogy competition by Sophocles

3. USHCOR = 3. _____
Group that sings and comments on the actions of the characters

4. DOLG = 4. _____
According to Creon, all prophets love this.

5. OENCR = 5. _____
Took over as King of Thebes after the war

6. AMN = 6. _____
___ is the most wonderful of all the world's wonders.

7. EUOPLOGR = 7. _____
Introduces the main characters at the beginning of the play

8. SONREA = 8. _____
God's crowning gift to man, according to Haimon

9. DPSARAO = 9. _____
Opening song as the chorus makes its entrance

10. ESTISRS =10. _____
Relationship between Antigone and Ismene

11. UYBR =11. _____
Creon decreed it illegal to ___ Polyneices.

12. HSEOT =12. _____
Attempt to appeal to one's sense of moral duty as persuasion

13. EHSTBE =13. _____
It has seven gates in a yawning ring.

14. TPSOHA =14. _____
Attempt to use emotion as a means of persuasion

JUGGLE LETTERS ANSWER KEY Antigone

1. TAYSR = 1. SATYR
   Play that comically portrayed mythological stories or poked fun at politics

2. YLSHUCSAE = 2. AESCHYLUS
   Greek playwright who was defeated in the tetralogy competition by Sophocles

3. USHCOR = 3. CHORUS
   Group that sings and comments on the actions of the characters

4. DOLG = 4. GOLD
   According to Creon, all prophets love this.

5. OENCR = 5. CREON
   Took over as King of Thebes after the war

6. AMN = 6. MAN
   ___ is the most wonderful of all the world's wonders.

7. EUOPLOGR = 7. PROLOGUE
   Introduces the main characters at the beginning of the play

8. SONREA = 8. REASON
   God's crowning gift to man, according to Haimon

9. DPSARAO = 9. PARADOS
   Opening song as the chorus makes its entrance

10. ESTISRS = 10. SISTERS
    Relationship between Antigone and Ismene

11. UYBR = 11. BURY
    Creon decreed it illegal to ___ Polyneices.

12. HSEOT = 12. ETHOS
    Attempt to appeal to one's sense of moral duty as persuasion

13. EHSTBE = 13. THEBES
    It has seven gates in a yawning ring.

14. TPSOHA = 14. PATHOS
    Attempt to use emotion as a means of persuasion

VOCABULARY RESOURCE MATERIALS

Antigone Vocabulary Word List

No.	Word	Clue/Definition
1.	ANARCHISTS	Those who reject all forms of coercive control and authority
2.	APHORISM	Tersely phrased statement of a truth or opinion; an adage
3.	ASTRAY	Away from the right or good; straying to or into wrong or evil ways
4.	AUGURY	Art, ability, or practice of making predictions
5.	AUSPICIOUS	Attended by favorable circumstances
6.	BARBARIC	Without civilizing influences
7.	BARROW	Large mound of earth or stones placed over a burial site
8.	BLASPHEMY	Profane act, utterance, or writing concerning God
9.	BRAWL	Noisy quarrel or fight
10.	BRAY	Loud, harsh sound resembling that of a donkey
11.	BRAZEN	Made of brass
12.	CALAMITY	Event that brings terrible loss; disaster
13.	CARRION	Feeding on dead and decaying flesh
14.	CITADEL	Fortress in a commanding position in or near a city
15.	CLEMENT	Inclined to be lenient or merciful
16.	COMPREHENSIVE	Marked by or showing extensive understanding
17.	COMPULSIVE	Having the capacity to exert a strong, irresistible influence on
18.	CONSIDER	Think carefully about
19.	CONTEMPT	Feeling or attitude of regarding someone or something as inferior
20.	DECREE	Authoritative order having the force of law
21.	DEFERENCE	Yielding to the opinion, wishes, or judgment of another
22.	DEFLECTS	Turns aside or causes to turn aside
23.	DEFY	Refuse to submit to or cooperate with
24.	DEMORALIZING	Undermining the confidence or morale of; dishearten
25.	DIRGES	Funeral hymns
26.	DIVINERS	Those who can predict the future
27.	DROWSE	To be half asleep
28.	EDDY	Current of water moving against the direction of the main current
29.	EDICT	Formal command
30.	EMBERS	Small, glowing pieces of coal or wood, as in a dying fire
31.	ENDURED	Bore with tolerance
32.	ENTRAILS	Internal organs, especially the intestines
33.	FOLLY	Lack of good sense, understanding, or foresight
34.	GALES	Very strong winds
35.	GLUT	Fill beyond capacity, especially with food
36.	IMPLACABLE	Impossible to placate or appease
37.	INSOLENCE	Rudeness or disrespect
38.	LAMENTATION	Cry of sorrow and grief
39.	LITHE	Marked by effortless grace
40.	MARSHAL	Military officer of the highest rank in some countries
41.	PERVERSE	Obstinately persisting in an error or fault; wrongly self-willed or stubborn
42.	PIETY	Quality of being pious or reverent
43.	PREVAIL	To be greater in strength or influence; triumph
44.	PROCLAMATION	Official, formal, public announcement
45.	PROW	Forward part of a ship's hull
46.	ROUSED	Excited, as to anger or action; stirred up
47.	SATED	Satisfied to excess
48.	SENTRIES	Guards, especially soldiers posted at a given spot to prevent the passage of unauthorized persons
49.	SLACKEN	Make or become less tense, taut, or firm; loosen
50.	SUBORDINATE	Subject to the authority or control of another

Antigone Vocabulary Word List

No.	Word	Clue/Definition
51.	SULTRY	Very humid and hot
52.	TORMENTED	Caused great physical pain or mental anguish
53.	TRANSCENDS	Passes beyond the limits of something
54.	TRANSGRESS	Commit an offense by violating a law or command; sin
55.	VENGEANCE	Infliction of punishment in return for a wrong committed
56.	VIGIL	Watch kept during normal sleeping hours
57.	VILE	Deserving of contempt or scorn
58.	WRETCHED	In a deplorable state of distress or misfortune
59.	YIELD	Give up (an advantage, for example) to another; concede

VOCABULARY WORD SEARCH Antigone

```
L A M E N T A T I O N C A L A M I T Y V
A C A R R I O N T R A N S C E N D S D Y
H J U L T S C S S L I A R T N E Z B E Y
S X G M W L R B T P M E T N O C L M T Q
R L U G E X W C R O U S E D A R L A R
A R R G N B R W E G T R A N S G R E S S
M E Y I R Z P C L N K Y V P P F R E E U
T L V F D M N R F R H F H M B V I L D B
Y I E L D E M B E R S E W O R R A B D O
D V D Y L V F D D V M D Z V T G A E Z R
S N A O J I I E V Y A V G N T P H Z J D
R R S S G S D V R Z Q I E T K C V P E I
B N N F N L E I S E Y S L Y T E I P P N
I D N O V U M S M V N D D E N D V R R A
E R C C I P O N D P L C R G F I O G O T
N O F L G M R E E L L W E S O C P R W E
D W K E I O A H C I T A D E L T J B T W
U S S M L C L E R K N N C A L A A J O J
R E E E T L I R E C R H M A Y R C R R R
E B G N G I Z P E Y J A Y V B X N K M D
D T R T N T I M F Q T A E A G L U T E H
Z N I A S H N O R I R R D S W E S N N
V J D M W E G C O T M I M D D H G K T G
K F X F J L R N S B C J C C K Y L Y E Y
S U L T R Y C A N A R C H I S T S Q D W
```

ANARCHISTS	CLEMENT	DROWSE	LITHE	TORMENTED
ASTRAY	COMPREHENSIVE	EDDY	MARSHAL	TRANSCENDS
AUGURY	COMPULSIVE	EDICT	PIETY	TRANSGRESS
BARBARIC	CONSIDER	EMBERS	PREVAIL	VENGEANCE
BARROW	CONTEMPT	ENDURED	PROCLAMATION	VIGIL
BLASPHEMY	DECREE	ENTRAILS	PROW	VILE
BRAWL	DEFERENCE	FOLLY	ROUSED	WRETCHED
BRAY	DEFLECTS	GALES	SATED	YIELD
BRAZEN	DEFY	GLUT	SENTRIES	
CALAMITY	DEMORALIZING	IMPLACABLE	SLACKEN	
CARRION	DIRGES	INSOLENCE	SUBORDINATE	
CITADEL	DIVINERS	LAMENTATION	SULTRY	

VOCABULARY WORD SEARCH ANSWER KEY Antigone

ANARCHISTS	CLEMENT	DROWSE	LITHE	TORMENTED
ASTRAY	COMPREHENSIVE	EDDY	MARSHAL	TRANSCENDS
AUGURY	COMPULSIVE	EDICT	PIETY	TRANSGRESS
BARBARIC	CONSIDER	EMBERS	PREVAIL	VENGEANCE
BARROW	CONTEMPT	ENDURED	PROCLAMATION	VIGIL
BLASPHEMY	DECREE	ENTRAILS	PROW	VILE
BRAWL	DEFERENCE	FOLLY	ROUSED	WRETCHED
BRAY	DEFLECTS	GALES	SATED	YIELD
BRAZEN	DEFY	GLUT	SENTRIES	
CALAMITY	DEMORALIZING	IMPLACABLE	SLACKEN	
CARRION	DIRGES	INSOLENCE	SUBORDINATE	
CITADEL	DIVINERS	LAMENTATION	SULTRY	

VOCABULARY CROSSWORD Antigone

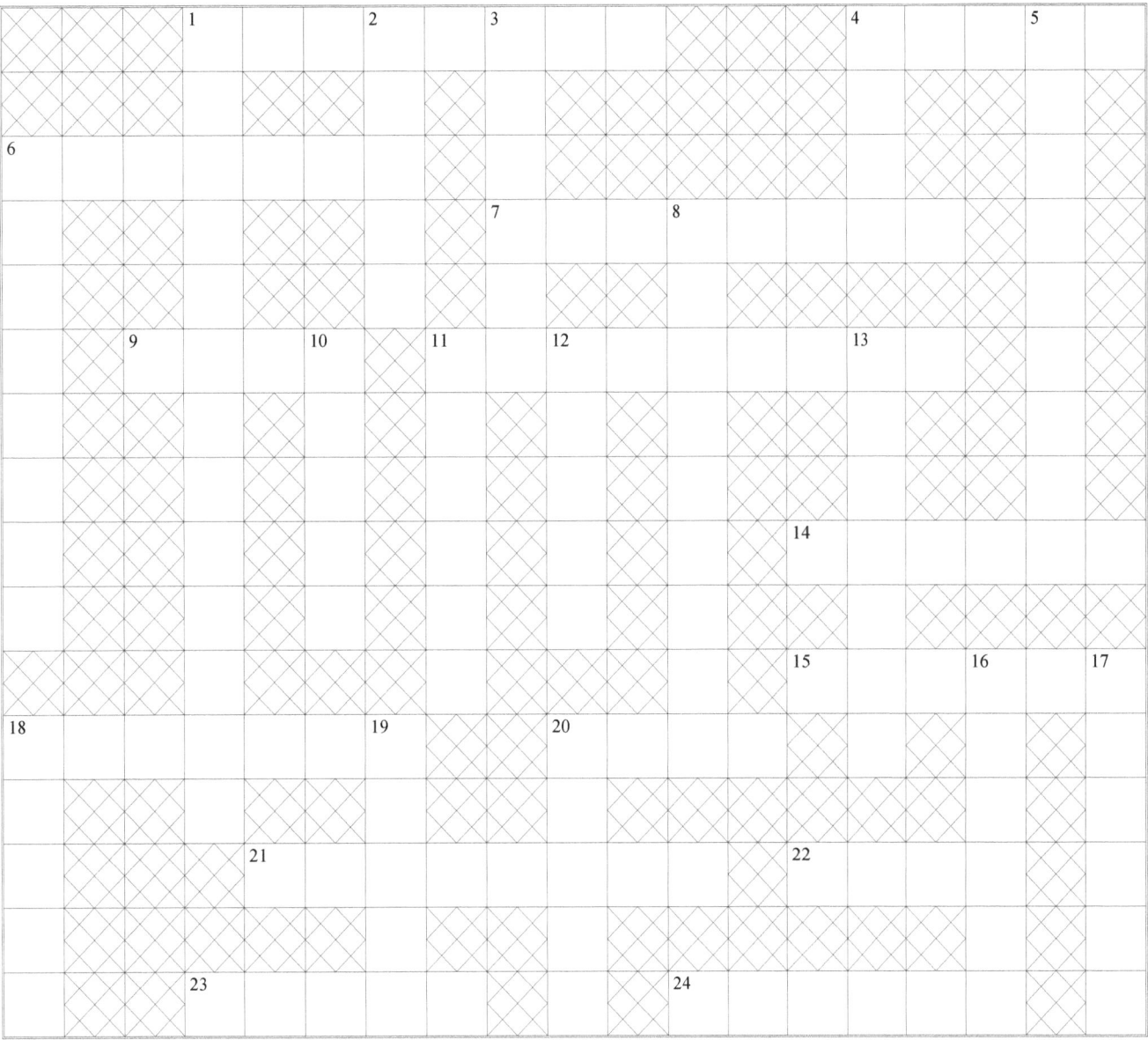

Across
1. Think carefully about
4. Watch kept during normal sleeping hours
6. Inclined to be lenient or merciful
7. In a deplorable state of distress or misfortune
9. Refuse to submit to or cooperate with
11. Yielding to the opinion, wishes, or judgment of another
14. Made of brass
15. Excited, as to anger or action; stirred up
18. To be greater in strength or influence; triumph
20. Current of water moving against the direction of the main current
21. Internal organs, especially the intestines
22. Fill beyond capacity, especially with food
23. Very strong winds
24. Away from the right or good; straying to or into wrong or evil ways

Down
1. Marked by or showing extensive understanding
2. Satisfied to excess
3. To be half asleep
4. Deserving of contempt or scorn
5. Rudeness or disrespect
6. Feeling or attitude of regarding someone or something as inferior
8. Caused great physical pain or mental anguish
10. Give up (an advantage, for example) to another; concede
11. Funeral hymns
12. Lack of good sense, understanding, or foresight
13. Feeding on dead and decaying flesh
16. Very humid and hot
17. Authoritative order having the force of law
18. Quality of being pious or reverent
19. Marked by effortless grace
20. Formal command

VOCABULARY CROSSWORD ANSWER KEY Antigone

		1 C	O	N	2 S	I	3 D	E	R		4 V	I	G	5 I	L
			O		A		R				I			N	
6 C	L	E	M	E	N	T		O			L			S	
O			P		E		7 W	R	E	8 T	C	H	E	D	
N			R		D		S			O				L	
T		9 D	E	10 F	Y	11 D	E	12 F	E	R	13 E	N	C	E	
E			H		I		I		O		M			A		N
M			E		E		R		L		E			R		C
P			N		L		G		L		N		14 B	R	A	Z	E	N
T			S		D		E		Y		T			I		
			I				S				E		15 R	O	16 U	S	E	17 D
18 P	R	E	V	A	I	19 L		20 E	D	D	Y		N		U		E
I			E			I			D						L		C
E					21 E	N	T	R	A	I	L	S		22 G	L	U	T	R
T						H			C								R	E
Y			23 G	A	L	E	S		24 A	S	T	R	A	Y				E

Across
1. Think carefully about
4. Watch kept during normal sleeping hours
6. Inclined to be lenient or merciful
7. In a deplorable state of distress or misfortune
9. Refuse to submit to or cooperate with
11. Yielding to the opinion, wishes, or judgment of another
14. Made of brass
15. Excited, as to anger or action; stirred up
18. To be greater in strength or influence; triumph
20. Current of water moving against the direction of the main current
21. Internal organs, especially the intestines
22. Fill beyond capacity, especially with food
23. Very strong winds
24. Away from the right or good; straying to or into wrong or evil ways

Down
1. Marked by or showing extensive understanding
2. Satisfied to excess
3. To be half asleep
4. Deserving of contempt or scorn
5. Rudeness or disrespect
6. Feeling or attitude of regarding someone or something as inferior
8. Caused great physical pain or mental anguish
10. Give up (an advantage, for example) to another; concede
11. Funeral hymns
12. Lack of good sense, understanding, or foresight
13. Feeding on dead and decaying flesh
16. Very humid and hot
17. Authoritative order having the force of law
18. Quality of being pious or reverent
19. Marked by effortless grace
20. Formal command

VOCABULARY MATCHING 1 Antigone

___ 1. DIRGES   A. To be half asleep
___ 2. PERVERSE   B. Those who reject all forms of coercive control and authority
___ 3. DECREE   C. Quality of being pious or reverent
___ 4. VIGIL   D. Watch kept during normal sleeping hours
___ 5. PROW   E. Undermining the confidence or morale of; dishearten
___ 6. SUBORDINATE   F. Formal command
___ 7. CARRION   G. Excited, as to anger or action; stirred up
___ 8. BRAY   H. Loud, harsh sound resembling that of a donkey
___ 9. CLEMENT   I. Authoritative order having the force of law
___10. EDDY   J. Those who can predict the future
___11. DROWSE   K. Art, ability, or practice of making predictions
___12. ROUSED   L. Cry of sorrow and grief
___13. EDICT   M. Deserving of contempt or scorn
___14. GALES   N. Obstinately persisting in an error or fault; wrongly self-willed or stubborn
___15. ANARCHISTS   O. Without civilizing influences
___16. DEFLECTS   P. Current of water moving against the direction of the main current
___17. DIVINERS   Q. Subject to the authority or control of another
___18. BARBARIC   R. Funeral hymns
___19. DEFY   S. Inclined to be lenient or merciful
___20. DEMORALIZING   T. Fortress in a commanding position in or near a city
___21. VILE   U. Very strong winds
___22. CITADEL   V. Refuse to submit to or cooperate with
___23. LAMENTATION   W. Feeding on dead and decaying flesh
___24. AUGURY   X. Turns aside or causes to turn aside
___25. PIETY   Y. Forward part of a ship's hull

VOCABULARY MATCHING 1 ANSWER KEY Antigone

R - 1. DIRGES — A. To be half asleep
N - 2. PERVERSE — B. Those who reject all forms of coercive control and authority
I - 3. DECREE — C. Quality of being pious or reverent
D - 4. VIGIL — D. Watch kept during normal sleeping hours
Y - 5. PROW — E. Undermining the confidence or morale of; dishearten
Q - 6. SUBORDINATE — F. Formal command
W - 7. CARRION — G. Excited, as to anger or action; stirred up
H - 8. BRAY — H. Loud, harsh sound resembling that of a donkey
S - 9. CLEMENT — I. Authoritative order having the force of law
P - 10. EDDY — J. Those who can predict the future
A - 11. DROWSE — K. Art, ability, or practice of making predictions
G - 12. ROUSED — L. Cry of sorrow and grief
F - 13. EDICT — M. Deserving of contempt or scorn
U - 14. GALES — N. Obstinately persisting in an error or fault; wrongly self-willed or stubborn
B - 15. ANARCHISTS — O. Without civilizing influences
X - 16. DEFLECTS — P. Current of water moving against the direction of the main current
J - 17. DIVINERS — Q. Subject to the authority or control of another
O - 18. BARBARIC — R. Funeral hymns
V - 19. DEFY — S. Inclined to be lenient or merciful
E - 20. DEMORALIZING — T. Fortress in a commanding position in or near a city
M - 21. VILE — U. Very strong winds
T - 22. CITADEL — V. Refuse to submit to or cooperate with
L - 23. LAMENTATION — W. Feeding on dead and decaying flesh
K - 24. AUGURY — X. Turns aside or causes to turn aside
C - 25. PIETY — Y. Forward part of a ship's hull

VOCABULARY MATCHING 2 Antigone

___ 1. ENTRAILS A. Those who can predict the future

___ 2. APHORISM B. Guards, especially soldiers posted at a given spot to prevent the passage of unauthorized persons

___ 3. EDDY C. Make or become less tense, taut, or firm; loosen

___ 4. DIVINERS D. Caused great physical pain or mental anguish

___ 5. CONTEMPT E. Feeling or attitude of regarding someone or something as inferior

___ 6. PROCLAMATION F. Authoritative order having the force of law

___ 7. EMBERS G. Lack of good sense, understanding, or foresight

___ 8. TORMENTED H. Refuse to submit to or cooperate with

___ 9. SENTRIES I. Very humid and hot

___ 10. SULTRY J. Official, formal, public announcement

___ 11. EDICT K. Formal command

___ 12. BRAWL L. Deserving of contempt or scorn

___ 13. PROW M. Art, ability, or practice of making predictions

___ 14. CALAMITY N. Noisy quarrel or fight

___ 15. DEFERENCE O. Turns aside or causes to turn aside

___ 16. DECREE P. Give up (an advantage, for example) to another; concede

___ 17. VILE Q. Event that brings terrible loss; disaster

___ 18. AUGURY R. Tersely phrased statement of a truth or opinion; an adage

___ 19. YIELD S. Forward part of a ship's hull

___ 20. DEFY T. Current of water moving against the direction of the main current

___ 21. TRANSCENDS U. Internal organs, especially the intestines

___ 22. SLACKEN V. Commit an offense by violating a law or command; sin

___ 23. DEFLECTS W. Yielding to the opinion, wishes, or judgment of another

___ 24. FOLLY X. Passes beyond the limits of something

___ 25. TRANSGRESS Y. Small, glowing pieces of coal or wood, as in a dying fire

VOCABULARY MATCHING 2 ANSWER KEY Antigone

U - 1. ENTRAILS	A.	Those who can predict the future
R - 2. APHORISM	B.	Guards, especially soldiers posted at a given spot to prevent the passage of unauthorized persons
T - 3. EDDY	C.	Make or become less tense, taut, or firm; loosen
A - 4. DIVINERS	D.	Caused great physical pain or mental anguish
E - 5. CONTEMPT	E.	Feeling or attitude of regarding someone or something as inferior
J - 6. PROCLAMATION	F.	Authoritative order having the force of law
Y - 7. EMBERS	G.	Lack of good sense, understanding, or foresight
D - 8. TORMENTED	H.	Refuse to submit to or cooperate with
B - 9. SENTRIES	I.	Very humid and hot
I - 10. SULTRY	J.	Official, formal, public announcement
K - 11. EDICT	K.	Formal command
N - 12. BRAWL	L.	Deserving of contempt or scorn
S - 13. PROW	M.	Art, ability, or practice of making predictions
Q - 14. CALAMITY	N.	Noisy quarrel or fight
W 15. DEFERENCE	O.	Turns aside or causes to turn aside
F - 16. DECREE	P.	Give up (an advantage, for example) to another; concede
L - 17. VILE	Q.	Event that brings terrible loss; disaster
M 18. AUGURY	R.	Tersely phrased statement of a truth or opinion; an adage
P - 19. YIELD	S.	Forward part of a ship's hull
H - 20. DEFY	T.	Current of water moving against the direction of the main current
X - 21. TRANSCENDS	U.	Internal organs, especially the intestines
C - 22. SLACKEN	V.	Commit an offense by violating a law or command; sin
O - 23. DEFLECTS	W.	Yielding to the opinion, wishes, or judgment of another
G - 24. FOLLY	X.	Passes beyond the limits of something
V - 25. TRANSGRESS	Y.	Small, glowing pieces of coal or wood, as in a dying fire

VOCABULARY JUGGLE LETTERS Antigone

1. ALBRW = 1. _____
   Noisy quarrel or fight

2. DEIYL = 2. _____
   Give up (an advantage, for example) to another; concede

3. OABWRR = 3. _____
   Large mound of earth or stones placed over a burial site

4. ZMEONIADLGRI = 4. _____
   Undermining the confidence or morale of; dishearten

5. PRWO = 5. _____
   Forward part of a ship's hull

6. MASHPIRO = 6. _____
   Tersely phrased statement of a truth or opinion; an adage

7. RSBEEM = 7. _____
   Small, glowing pieces of coal or wood, as in a dying fire

8. ALTYCAMI = 8. _____
   Event that brings terrible loss; disaster

9. TSRCHIANAS = 9. _____
   Those who reject all forms of coercive control and authority

10. UDRTEOABNIS = 10. _____
    Subject to the authority or control of another

11. EUOSRD = 11. _____
    Excited, as to anger or action; stirred up

12. IEESEMONHPVCR = 12. _____
    Marked by or showing extensive understanding

13. OCNIERDS = 13. _____
    Think carefully about

14. LFYOL = 14. _____
    Lack of good sense, understanding, or foresight

VOCABULARY JUGGLE LETTERS ANSWER KEY Antigone

1. ALBRW = 1. BRAWL
   Noisy quarrel or fight

2. DEIYL = 2. YIELD
   Give up (an advantage, for example) to another; concede

3. OABWRR = 3. BARROW
   Large mound of earth or stones placed over a burial site

4. ZMEONIADLGRI = 4. DEMORALIZING
   Undermining the confidence or morale of; dishearten

5. PRWO = 5. PROW
   Forward part of a ship's hull

6. MASHPIRO = 6. APHORISM
   Tersely phrased statement of a truth or opinion; an adage

7. RSBEEM = 7. EMBERS
   Small, glowing pieces of coal or wood, as in a dying fire

8. ALTYCAMI = 8. CALAMITY
   Event that brings terrible loss; disaster

9. TSRCHIANAS = 9. ANARCHISTS
   Those who reject all forms of coercive control and authority

10. UDRTEOABNIS =10. SUBORDINATE
    Subject to the authority or control of another

11. EUOSRD =11. ROUSED
    Excited, as to anger or action; stirred up

12. IEESEMONHPVCR =12. COMPREHENSIVE
    Marked by or showing extensive understanding

13. OCNIERDS =13. CONSIDER
    Think carefully about

14. LFYOL =14. FOLLY
    Lack of good sense, understanding, or foresight

www.ingramcontent.com/pod-product-compliance
Lightning Source LLC
LaVergne TN
LVHW081536060526
838200LV00048B/2092